THE
DAY
BEFORE
ETERNITY

THE

DAY

BEFORE

ETERNITY

ROD PARSLEY

CREATION HOUSE

THE DAY BEFORE ETERNITY by Rod Parsley
Published by Creation House
Strang Communications Company
600 Rinehart Road
Lake Mary, Florida 32746
Web site: http://www.creationhouse.com

Unless otherwise noted, all Scripture quotations are
from the King James Version of the Bible.

Scripture quotations marked NKJV are from the New
King James Version of the Bible. Copyright © 1979, 1980, 1982
by Thomas Nelson, Inc., publishers. Used by permission.

Scripture quotations marked NAS are from the New American Standard
Bible. Copyright © 1960, 1962, 1963, 1968, 1971, 1972, 1973, 1975,
1977 by the Lockman Foundation. Used by permission.

Scripture quotations marked NIV are from the Holy Bible,
New International Version. Copyright © 1973, 1978, 1984,
International Bible Society. Used by permission.

Library of Congress Cataloging-in-Publication Data
Parsley, Rod.
The day before eternity / Rod Parsley.
p. cm.
ISBN 0-88419-574-0
1. Christian life. I. Title
BV4501.2.P35235 1998
243—dc21   98-45970
                                                                   CIP

8 9 0 1 2 3 4 5 BVG 8 7 6 5 4 3 2 1

Printed in the United States of America

*Sometimes there aren't enough words
to adequately express the impact that
someone close to you has upon your life.
This is the way that I feel about my parents,*
James and Ellen Parsley.

From the time I was a small child, my parents have always raised me in the nurture and admonition of the Lord. When I felt the tugging of the Holy Spirit upon my heart at age eight, my parents questioned my intent for going to the altar. My response was, "I am a sinner, and I need a Savior." It was the right answer, and at that moment I gave my life completely to Jesus.

When I received my first allowance, my mother and father sat me down and taught me that ten cents of every dollar belonged to God as my tithe. Because of their biblical teaching and their example, I cannot recall an instance where they or I did not tithe and give offerings.

I never remember a time when my parents missed a service or allowed me to miss one to play in a basketball game, which I loved, or any other thing for that matter. Being in the house of God every time the doors were opened and developing a deep and intimate relationship with Him was the most important thing to them. Through their example, this same desire was instilled in me as well.

When I first felt the call to be a pastor at the age of nineteen, my parents encouraged me to follow the leading of the Holy Spirit. It never ceased to amaze me the sacrifices they continually made on my behalf to allow me to follow God's calling upon my life. They have stood as immovable bulwarks alongside my wife, Joni, and me—not only during times of great victory but also in times of great challenge and adversity.

I thank God every day for my wonderful parents and for the unique opportunity to serve together with them in His kingdom.

They have raised me to know and serve God and to honor and respect the men and women of God. They are true Christians who have led by example and have instructed me in the things of God my entire life. I believe the words in Proverbs 22:6 say it best: "Train up a child in the way he should go: and when he is old, he will not depart from it."

Mom and Dad, thank you for listening, caring, encouraging, correcting, and believing in me. Your unconditional love for God and me has left an indelible print upon my heart; I will never be the same.

CONTENTS

THE DAY BEFORE ETERNITY DAWNS

Morning is dawning on the last day before eternity.

On the distant horizon a cloud of glory appears and advances across a dusty, dry desert. Unlike anything that has been, the thunderous cloud approaches. As if being trodden under by millions of hoofbeats, the ground shakes with an earthquake that cannot be silenced. That cloud of glory crushes every enemy underfoot as it relentlessly moves toward eternity's dawn.

Ahead of the cloud rides the King of glory on a white horse, radiant as the sun and beautiful as the moon. A terrible army marching under His banner follows His lead into history's last day and final hours.

What is this cloud of glory?
Who is this King of glory?
Why has a thundering march commenced?
What will happen on this last day before eternity?
How will it affect and change you and me?

This book will answer each question. But before we begin marching through this last day and its final hours, permit me to pull back the curtains and give you a brief glimpse, a quick snapshot of this terrible army, this cloud of glory called the *ecclesia,* which marches undaunted into eternity.

THE REMNANT, REVOLUTIONARY CHURCH

Marching across the desert of time and into the eternal river of glory, the *ecclesia*—Christ's true church—comes out of the dark and into the light.

At Pentecost, the *ecclesia* was birthed but not fulfilled, betrothed but not wedded, engaged but not consummated. The Bridegroom is yet to come for a bride without spot or blemish.

In Acts 2, when the day of Pentecost was fully come, they were all together in one accord. Notice that *all* doesn't mean all of those called out of natural Israel into a royal priesthood and a holy nation. All who were called were not there. At least six hundred received the invitation to be there, but only one hundred twenty showed up.

God was ready to pour out His Spirit and fulfill the prophecy of Joel:

> I will pour out my spirit upon all flesh; and your sons and your daughters shall prophesy, your old men shall dream dreams, your young men shall see visions: And also upon the servants and upon the handmaids in those days will I pour out my spirit.
>
> —JOEL 2:28–29

The shocking truth is that God did not pour out His Spirit on all flesh then, and since the day of Pentecost we've been looking for something that has not yet come.

God did not pour out His Spirit on Jerusalem.

God did not pour out His Spirit on the six hundred whom He had invited to be in the upper room.

God poured out His Spirit, not on the nation of Israel, not on the city of Jerusalem, not on the six hundred who were invited, but God poured out His Spirit on one hundred twenty individuals who had gathered themselves in humble obedience in an upper room in Jerusalem.

God poured out His Spirit upon a people within a people . . . on a nation within a nation . . . and on a church within a church.

Until this day before eternity, the *ecclesia* has been a remnant, ragtag band of soldiers. It is much like the shabby army that George Washington gathered at Valley Forge during the winter of the Revolutionary War, when the bleakest and darkest hours of the war foreboded defeat for the young, infant people laboring to be birthed as a nation.

But defeat wasn't in Washington's vocabulary—nor is it in ours. This remnant, revolutionary church is the called-out body—the *ecclesia*—that is light in darkness . . . salt in the insipid world . . . new wine splitting old wineskins . . . and holiness blazing a fiery trial of morality in the midst of the dregs of worldly immorality and lust.

Ecclesia is the army within an army . . . the river within a river . . . the faithful among the faithless . . . and the wheat amidst the tares.

Cultural Christianity has become a cult of the comfortable and the complacent. It is the institutional church whether it calls itself denominational or nondenominational; pentecostal or cessationist; evangelical or liberal; traditional or contemporary. Like a silent cancer destroying vital organs before ever detected by an MRI, cultic, institutional Christianity has polluted the river of God and made a sacrilege of His holiness and purity.

Cultural Christianity has lost its *distinctiveness*—one cannot tell the so-called church from the world or the saints from the sinners.

Cultural Christianity has lost its *vitality*—a corpse poses as a body dancing like a marionette being manipulated by a worldly puppeteer whose power comes from the prince of darkness.

Cultural Christianity has lost *Jesus*. Yes, He is talked about and in His name people cast out devils and prophesy, but they do not *know* Him. The knowledge and the fear of God has been lost in this religious cult where style substitutes for substance; haughtiness pushes aside holiness; lust masquerades as love; performance poses as presence; and pretense subverts truth.

But this dry season of deadening, numbing religion will be swept away in a cloud of glory on this last day before eternity.

In this final day, there will be *no dry season* and *no more crumbs!* The latter rain and the former rain will fall in the same month. The reaper will overtake the sower.

And God's Spirit will be poured out upon all flesh.

In this day before eternity, the remnant church will become the revolutionary church rebelling against all religion and overcoming every enemy. No weapon formed against this mighty army will prosper (Isa. 54:17). No one within this body of Christ will go untouched by the Spirit of God being poured forth as new wine.

- Are you ready for the day before eternity?
- Are you ready to eat bread you have never tasted and drink new wine you have never drunk?
- Are you ready to feel what you have never felt and live what before now had only been but a dream?
- Are you ready to swim in a river described in Ezekiel 47 that will not only rise up to your ankles, knees, or waist but will flood your being with rivers of living water?
- Are you ready for a church, a called-out people, who look the devil in the eye and put him beneath their heels where he is crushed and overcome?

In this last day before eternity, God is preparing a people—the *ecclesia*—who will march as a cloud of glory into the dawn of eternity. This book is a trumpet call to prepare you to be that church of the living God marching with the King of glory into eternal victory.

Are you ready?

Today is the day before eternity!

 **ONE**

MARCHING IN GOD'S REVOLUTIONARY ARMY

For whosoever will save his life shall lose it: but whosoever will lose his life for my sake, the same shall save it.

—LUKE 9:24

Throughout the day before eternity, a revolution burns like a desert wildfire consuming everything in its path. At the forefront of this revolutionary war marches the church in step with her Commander in Chief, Jesus Christ.

During America's Revolutionary War, marriages, educations, jobs, and personal pursuits were put on hold for the good of birthing democracy in the New World. Like America's early citizens, we too are putting personal priorities on hold in order to fulfill eternal mandates. However, there is a difference between America's Revolutionary War and this all-consuming fire raging in this last day before eternity.

In the American Revolution, one might lose one's life forever to the temporal cause of democracy. But in this last-day war, everyone who loses his life for the Commander's sake will find it. "For whosoever will save his life shall lose it: but whosoever will lose his life for my sake, the same shall save it" (Luke 9:24).

This war that rages in the final day before eternity has a specific battle plan. First, the enemy has been identified and his strategies unmasked. "Put on the whole armour of God, that ye may be able to stand against the wiles of the devil" (Eph. 6:11). The enemy is Satan, whose tactics culminate in accusing the saints (Rev. 12:10).

Second, the revolution's outcome has already been determined. While the outcome of the American Revolution hung in the balance for months, the outcome of this final-day revolutionary war has already been revealed. The army of saints in the true church of Jesus Christ will overcome and defeat Satan. He will be cast into a lake of everlasting fire for eternity (Rev. 20).

Third and finally, we must be prepared to wage war. Our lazy, nonchalant attitude toward evangelism, conversion, repentance, revival, renewal, and holiness must be radically changed and altered by God. The revolution will go on with or without us. We will either fight or be trampled underfoot by a mighty, holy army of God that refuses to retreat, surrender, or even pause in its forward advance.

For those who shrink back in their pursuit, the church of the living God will pass you by, and your eternal reward will become a charred rubble (1 Cor. 3:12–15).

Are you ready for the revolution? Have you prepared for the last day before eternity? How do you enlist in this awesome army that marches "fair as the moon, clear as the sun, and terrible as an army with banners" (Song of Sol. 6:10)? Into some armies soldiers are drafted. For others, soldiers volunteer. But the only way to enter the Lord's army, which is waging a terrible battle during this last day, is to surrender—radically surrender to the Lord of the battle, the King of kings, Jesus Christ.

RADICAL SURRENDER

During the last days before his eternity, a friend of mine discovered radical surrender. He was a huge fellow and had been a member of the notorious Hells' Angels motorcycle gang.

He lived on eternity's edge. His violent lifestyle put him on the precipice of death constantly. He would do things such as take a man into the restroom of a bar to shoot both of his kneecaps simply because that fellow had made him angry. Once while in prison, he spent forty days in solitary confinement in a six-by-six-by-eight-foot "hole," where he broke all the bones in his fingers and hands by beating his fists against the cell walls. When the guards came and returned him to a regular cell, they noticed his broken fingers and compounded the pain by smashing his hands with a hammer.

On this side of eternity, this man was the last person you would want to meet in a dark alley. But after his radical surrender, you could trust him with your bank account, car, family, and anything you could ask him to do. What is radical surrender? Totally surrendering one's life to the one who reigns in eternity—Jesus!

One day my friend visited a few of us who were sitting on the porch of our first church building. I asked him, "What would you do if somebody came up to you right now and popped you in the mouth?"

"I honestly believe with all my heart," he responded, "that I'd just look him in the eye, tell him I loved him, and pat him on the back."

My mother was struggling with some physical problems during the time of his visit, and when he found out about it, that gentle giant sought her out, laid hands on her, and prayed for her healing. His huge hands could palm a basketball. They were thick and hard, but my mother will tell you she had never felt anything more gentle than this massive man's huge hands.

Jesus Christ has the power to take a burly, destructive gangster like my friend and transform him into a minister of the gospel. His radical surrender infused his life with God's love. This man who once lived for Satan was filled with the Spirit of God, which in turn gave him a peace and direction he had never known.

MOVE FROM TIME INTO ETERNITY

Buddha, Muhammad, or Krishna could not have done this for my friend, for me, or for you. The millions who have surrendered to their philosophies and religion receive just that—philosophy and religion. I like the bumper stickers often seen around Christmas time, "Wise Men Still Seek Him." In this last day before eternity we need to possess enough wisdom to do one thing right—seek the only One who can save and change our lives.

Jesus Christ is the only One who has the power to give us new life. Whomever the Son sets free is free indeed, because Jesus became flesh and dwelt among us to give us eternal life (John 8:36; 1:14). Everyone in the End-Time army must be set free by Jesus.

Jesus doesn't require the hard works of fruitless religion. We don't have to pay thousands of dollars to travel to "holy" earthly places to throw rocks at stone pillars representing Satan, wash in the "holy" rivers, shave our heads, or grow a beard. Only one response is required by God—radical surrender. When we surrender, Jesus sends the Holy Spirit to restore us to life.

Jesus Christ will give you a hundred reasons for living when dying looks easy, if you'll just let Him. Remember: He's not mad at you. He loves you and gave His life for you, and He's coming back to this earth to receive you unto Himself! There isn't anything more self-destructive than rejecting His gracious offer of pardon and new life.

To resist Jesus Christ is to reject Him. The Bible says that every time people say *no* to an invitation to receive Him as their sovereign Lord, their hearts become calloused, "having their conscience seared with a hot iron" (1 Tim. 4:2).

Once you have resisted Jesus, it will be easier to resist Him the next time He knocks at your heart. Finally your heart will become so calloused and hard that you will no longer hear His gentle knock at your heart's door.

If you have already received Jesus as Savior, allow Him to keep knocking on the door of your heart. Stay surrendered and allow Him to show you what He wants you to do. Jesus has the answer for whatever you're going through.

If you haven't received Jesus yet, pause right now and let down all your defenses. Why not stop running? Why not say *yes* to God? Before you turn another page, you can surrender your life to Jesus and be filled with the Holy Spirit's power to change your life. He will change you from the inside out, and this book will be your initial guide into the day before eternity.

Are you ready? Pray aloud with complete and radical surrender:

Father God, I repent of my sins right now before You and ask You to forgive me, a sinner, through the sacrificial offering and blood of Jesus Christ. I surrender all to You now, in Jesus' name, and I promise to follow You all the days of my life. I pray this, heavenly Father, in Jesus' name. Amen.

If you prayed this prayer for the first time, I want to welcome you to the family of God. The Bible says that even now the angels of heaven are rejoicing with your decision! So am I! Now I invite you to say, "I'm going to serve God and not the devil. I'm going to live life and experience God's blessing, not the devil's cursing."

Welcome! You are now ready to be alive on the day before the end, the day before eternity. The Second Coming of Christ is now nearer than ever, and you are ready because of your total and radical surrender to Him.

Scripture declares, "If any man walk in the day, he stumbleth not, because he seeth the light of this world. But if a man walk in the night, he stumbleth, because there is no light in him" (John 11:9–10). And this could have been my friend, or you, if you hadn't surrendered your life to Christ.

ABUNDANT LIFE

In the last day, radical surrender brings to us an abundant life. John 10:10 says, "The thief cometh not, but for to steal, and to kill, and to destroy: I am come that they might have life, and that they might have it more abundantly."

The radical surrender of a soul begins with receiving Jesus Christ's new, eternal life, and it ends with receiving an even newer, higher form of life. Paul says that to be absent from the body is to be present with the Lord (2 Cor. 5:8). What awaits mankind's born-again spirit in the heavenlies beyond physical death far exceeds living on earth as mere mortals with eternity in our hearts.

There is another exciting level of life awaiting all who have surrendered their lives to Christ. On a day no one knows but our heavenly Father, God is going to change the mortal flesh in which we now live into a body like the one Jesus received when God raised Him from the dead. There is a rapture coming for all who love God and a resurrection of the body for every saint who has already moved on to heaven.

When Jesus surrendered His life on the cross, He became our resurrected down payment as the firstborn from the dead to purchase this greater, abundant life. The Bible declares Jesus is the firstfruits of another age to come after this world and our present church age have ended.

> But now is Christ risen from the dead, and become the first-fruits of them that slept. For since by man came death, by man came also the resurrection of the dead. For as in Adam all die, even so in Christ shall all be made alive.
> —1 CORINTHIANS 15:20–22

In other words, because Jesus was raised from the dead, those who have accepted Him will also be raised from the dead. And if Jesus was raptured as the Word of God declares, then we have the promise that we will be raptured as well. Jesus Christ is the Son of God! And it was the Father's good pleasure to come down in Him to right the plague of sin that Adam's transgression allowed on the earth. From the moment that our true and living God shed the animal skins in the garden to cover Adam and Eve's sin with blood, He has been drawing men back to the eternal state in which Adam once lived and moved.

The man or woman who would surrender under God's Old Covenant could receive, through obeying the Law, a legal pardon and eventually go to Paradise (Abraham's bosom) after death.

Today under our New, and better, Covenant, we who have surrendered to Jesus Christ are re-created in our inner beings and ascend to God's dwelling in heaven at the body's death.

But there is coming a day—the last day before eternity—when death will be no more. In that coming day, all who have surrendered to God's love through Christ will receive another divine life change. And since the dark day of Adam's transgression in the garden, God has been fulfilling this, according to His time:

> But every man in his own order: Christ the firstfruits; after-
> ward they that are Christ's at his coming. Then cometh the
> end, when he shall have delivered up the kingdom to God,
> even the Father; when he shall have put down all rule and all
> authority and power. For he must reign, till he hath put all
> enemies under his feet. The last enemy that shall be destroyed
> is death.
>
> —1 CORINTHIANS 15:23–26

God wills that every human being be given the time and truth necessary to prepare for this powerful transition that will occur at the last ticking moment before time as we know it ceases to be. For those who are unprepared, eternal separation meted out by the Judge they rejected as King awaits them with the devil and his followers, eternally in hell. In this life, there is a heaven to be gained, and a hell to be shunned.

By the time anyone faces eternity, less than a hundred years has usually passed. This is less than one-tenth of what Scripture reveals as the length of one of God's days: "But, beloved, be not ignorant of this one thing, that one day is with the Lord as a thousand years, and a thousand years as one day" (2 Pet. 3:8). So for each of us, life is but a vapor that appears and fades away. Life is simply the last day before eternity!

TIME IS RUNNING OUT

History is currently plummeting madly into midnight, unaware that the Judge is coming to end life on earth as we now know it! Men and women scurry around as in the days of Noah before God judged the world some forty-four hundred years ago. Jesus said of that time that they were eating and drinking and giving in marriage, until one day when life as they knew it was over—and everyone except for Noah's family was drowned in the Great Flood (Matt. 24:38–39)!

A revolutionary church is marching with the divine purpose to change the world. It does not seek political or economic change. It does not battle for land or possessions. Rather, the change sought is in the hearts of men and women from every culture and strata of society. Change is not an option; it's a mandate. Without changed hearts, the human race will rush maddeningly through the gates of hell.

Everyone is raving today about the American economy. But the highest tax rates in U. S. history are forcing most marriage partners to race around at breakneck speeds to simply make ends meet. The remote lifestyles produced by the media and the druglike numbness of our culture's materialism have enslaved many Americans in a dreamlike state so that they have no clue as to the lateness of the hour. Surrender to them is defeat by life's odds. As the blood-bought, born-again, overcoming church, we need to sound the alarm and wake the world up to the reality that *this is the last day before eternity!*

When someone radically surrenders in this day before eternity, he becomes a lover, not a hater; a soulwinner, not a lost soul; a healer, not a destroyer. All those who are saved will be ready on the last day before eternity, because their changed hearts belong to Jesus, and they now love to share God's love with others.

We need to be more concerned about ministering to the needs of our lost loved ones and neighbors than caring for our own temporal needs. At the church I pastor, World Harvest Church, we are growing in every outreach program to bring Jesus to the people instead of expecting them to come to us. We're feeding the hungry and ministering to the poor.

Thousands are saved through television each year, so we're reaching out to get on more and more stations, bringing Jesus Christ into living rooms.

How about you? Do you know someone today who is aimlessly spinning their wheels trying to make things happen and are completely oblivious to the nearness of the return of Christ? Whether you just received Jesus as Savior or have known Him for years, if you know someone who has no idea of the times we're living in, start praying and asking God how you can reach them. Spend time with the unsaved people around you so that you can share God's love and lead them to Christ. This is the last day before eternity!

Start praying about how you can develop some new relationships. When Jesus met the Samaritan woman at the well, He talked to her about everyday concerns such as wells and water. But before He was done, the woman discovered who He was and what He had to offer, and she raced back to her town to tell everyone about Jesus.

Abundant life is meeting Jesus and living daily in His abundance. It is when we so overflow with His abundance that everyone around us meets Jesus and discovers through us about abundant and eternal life in Him.

CONTINUAL SURRENDER

Once we as God's people have accepted His unconditional pardon and new life in Jesus Christ, He expects our continual surrender to see salvation's race victoriously through to the end.

When John the Baptist paved Christ's way, he cried out in the wilderness, "Repent ye: for the kingdom of heaven is at hand" (Matt. 3:2). In essence he was saying, "Surrender, for the kingdom of God is near! Change your mind and purpose! Be sorry for your disobedient ways!" Since I have been saved and filled with God's Spirit, I've passed up a number of well-packaged opportunities to go back to my old way of thinking. I've refused many deceptive ploys to reject God's plan and purpose in my life and to run out and do my own thing. This is one of the ways Satan beguiles God's servants. He packages his lies in self-serving deceptions and temptations to destroy the work of God.

But thank God for His Holy Spirit, because without His presence in our lives, neither you nor I would have the unction for surrender. Without continual obedience, our lives would be entangled with pride and spiritual arrogance or self-righteousness.

It is the Holy Ghost's assignment to rescue every human on earth and bring them into fellowship with God—and He only moves and works in the lives of those who answer His call. All others who turn a deaf ear to His gentle tugging seek a religious experience to justify their sins. The Holy Spirit grieves over the millions upon millions of Muslims, Hindus, Buddhists, Mormons, Jehovah's

Witnesses, and other false religions that Satan initiated to deceive men into working their way to hell. Their lives may be filled with good works, but they are hopelessly lost in their sins.

False surrender brings people to a man—like Brigham Young, Joseph Smith, Muhammad, Confucius, or Buddha—or simply pagan-made metal, wood, and stone. Millions have surrendered to the master of deception. And the Holy Spirit, though touched by their passion to worship gods, must pass over them in His grief, to fill and minister to those who radically surrender to Him.

But did you know there are many strivers, doers, and workers in the born-again Christian church who in their own way are seeking a religious experience instead of a daily walk with Jesus? I don't mean to insinuate that the "religious" among our ranks aren't born again. What I do mean is that those who struggle through their day without surrendering to the Spirit's help are among our ranks. And, just as He passes over those false religions, the Holy Spirit must pass over their works-oriented attempts to please God. Why? Because the Holy Ghost's assignment is to those who seek His help and guidance. He isn't forced into doing anything, and He forces no one. He guides and leads those whose hearts are receptive to His leadings.

Possibly you are born again, but you do not sense the Holy Spirit's presence as you once did. Maybe the sweet anointing that you experienced in being born again has waxed cold or lukewarm. Perhaps you no longer zealously yearn to tell everyone you meet about Jesus. God wants to infuse you again with His Spirit so you can return to your first love and fall passionately in love again with Jesus.

QUIT STRIVING

If you find yourself simply going through the motions of being religious, the first thing you must decide is to *quit striving*. You must stop saying, "I have done all I'm capable of doing." Radical surrender is all of Jesus and none of me. It gives Him all the glory and takes no glory for self. Radical surrender says that He must increase and I must decrease. It stops trying and starts trusting Jesus for everything in life.

You were created with the purpose to glorify and live for God—this is the chief end of man. In the next chapter we will explore God's redemptive plan of the ages in which you are a vessel of praise, worship, service, and ministry. You are a piece of clay to be molded according to His plan. But when you strive on your own, you refuse the Potter's water that makes the clay pliable for His creative and restorative work. This is why Paul writes, "Nay but, O man, who art thou that repliest against God? Shall the thing formed say to him that formed it, Why hast thou made me thus?" (Rom. 9:20).

So many Christians today are racing along in the world's breakneck pace in order to make ends meet, and they rush right through their week without taking any private time with the "Potter" in devotional study or prayer. Church meetings are on their agenda. They show up smiling and ready to participate. I see them every week. But they're so burdened down from the stress of their striving that they can't get off the spiritual treadmill on which they are running.

Yes, they are devoted to church, ritual, meetings, services, good works, and trying hard to please God. But they are walking through these last days feeling unfulfilled and unused by God.

"I just can't do anything about this. I've come to the end of myself," I often hear them say when their treadmills finally break down. And this is good, because when they finally realize their religious calisthenics and breakfast-table prayer cards have been doing them no good, they wind up on the bottom. And that's a good place to be. Because it is at the bottom that you fall into the everlasting arms of the Potter. At the bottom, you must wait for the Holy Spirit to come alongside you as the *Paraclete,* the *Comforter,* to guide and restore you.

The Holy Spirit is the only One who can lift spiritual burdens. He is the only One who can put us in contact with the true, living God and then help us grow as true worshipers every day. Jesus told the woman at the well, "But the hour cometh, and now is, when the true worshippers shall worship the Father in spirit and in truth: for the Father seeketh such to worship him" (John 4:23). The church is called out of natural circumstances as a supernatural people to live "by the Spirit" in spite of our circumstances!

THE HOLY SPIRIT HAS BEEN WHERE YOU CAN'T GO

The Holy Spirit will help His people when we cry out for deliverance and petition the Father because He has been where we can't go. When you, as a child of God, cry out to the Father and present your requests to Him, the Holy Spirit is present in the throne room as a partner in God's counsel for your every need. The Holy Ghost hears your prayers, and He hears God's answer to minister to you twenty-four hours a day. Only He can lift your burdens and encourage you.

Pray and stay in the Word. To hear for yourself God's counsel, you must be a worshiper in Spirit and truth. That means your devotion in prayer and quiet time with Him to gain His mind for everything you may encounter. We can often find God's answers to our situations by simply reading His Word under the guidance of the Holy Spirit, who inspired the Word (2 Tim. 3:16). The woman at the well knew the Law of Moses, but she did not have a revelation of the Lawgiver. "Our fathers worshipped in this mountain; and ye say, that in Jerusalem is the place where men ought to worship" (John 4:20). In spite of the truth, she worshiped in the wrong place.

Striving like the Spirit-less religions of the world to worship on Mount Samaria is fruitless. Prayer wheels, bowing five times a day, or even a grand church building—void of God's leading and divine insight—is worship outside of the truth. True worshipers in Spirit and in truth will daily consult God's Word, His inspired, inerrant Scriptures.

They will spend quiet time to feel the sweet embrace of the One who condescends to men of low estate in a time of devoted prayer. "Thou wilt keep him in perfect peace, whose mind is stayed on thee: because he trusteth in thee" (Isa. 26:3).

Daily live a surrendered life. True worshipers of God will go about their daily affairs in a surrendered lifestyle with the Holy Spirit's counsel and comfort to keep them in perfect peace.

When surrender becomes a lifestyle for believers, the Holy Spirit will help them live abundantly every day.

As time slips away toward that last day before eternity, God is calling the world and His beloved bride, the church, to abandonment. He is moving feverishly through His blood-bought people around the world to bring as many as will to surrender their lives and accomplish His will.

When the bamboo curtain lifted in China several years ago, the world saw that God's people had flourished and mushroomed in underground church groups. Why? Because Hudson Taylor's Inland China Mission and following missionary successors such as Eric Liddle, of *Chariots of Fire* fame, had called the masses to a place of surrender. The brutal, repressive Chinese government couldn't stomp out the burning embers of the Holy Spirit's flames.

This was true for the first-century church when they spread out from Jerusalem to Samaria and then to the uttermost parts of the earth. Everywhere the enemy attempted to stamp out God's fire, the embers flew up and scattered from Jerusalem to Rome. Paul was "aborted" from his murderous mission on the Damascus Road because of the prayers of Christ's church. Saul, the Christian-killer, became the Holy Spirit's torchbearer—and the church exploded around the world as he proclaimed the good news of Jesus Christ. Paul announced to King Agrippa, "Whereupon, O king Agrippa, I was not disobedient unto the heavenly vision: but shewed first unto them of Damascus, and at Jerusalem, and throughout all the coasts of Judaea, and then to the Gentiles, that they should repent [surrender] and turn to God, and do works meet for [surrendered] repentance" (Acts 26:19–20).

When the prayers and acts of God's surrendered people behind Europe's iron curtain were answered, He tore down Communism's walls. And when He did, thousands rushed in to join those who had been ministering underground to find the fires of the Holy Spirit crackling in huge, engulfing flames.

Africa is ablaze today in great revival because of surrendered hearts around the huge continent that could house the land space of most modern countries.

Even the most difficult ground in the Middle East, which many have termed the 1040 window and where Islam, Hinduism, and Buddhism have established such strongholds, is feeling the rumblings of God's praying, active church today.

Surrender is not an option for those who would accept the free gift of Christ's sacrificial life, those who have named His name and received eternal life. If Jesus was resurrected, we too will be raised from the dead. And if Jesus was raptured, we too will be raptured when He returns. But it is also true that if Jesus humbled Himself in an act of obedience, we too must humble ourselves. Without complete abandonment to the cause of Christ, we receive very little victory and very little light, because the Holy Spirit enlightens the humble of heart.

DON'T PUT OUT THE LIGHT!

My grandfather lived in a little two-room Eastern Kentucky shack that was lit with kerosene lamps. As long as there was kerosene feeding into the wicks, those lamps would fill his house with light. But occasionally, he would forget to fill one; when he did, the lamp would still burn, but it wouldn't burn as it was intended to. The wick would catch fire because of the lack of fuel, and black smoke would fill his house, burning his eyes and producing a hideous odor in the air. When this happened, the lamp became a confusing cloud of smoke unable to light the way.

I think this illustration makes a good point of where we are missing God's Spirit today in the church. We aren't replenishing our oil. Like Eli of old, we are neglecting the lamps in the tabernacles of our hearts; too many among us are burning out for a lack of fuel. The end result to our burning is a haze of smoke. And when the smoke clears, nothing and no one has changed.

For years now, the status quo church has had the misconception that numeric growth was what God was after and that if we could just grow larger, we would have a greater influence on our generation. But we've been wrong!

Look around! Bigger doesn't necessarily mean better when we have unsurrendered, anonymous believers slipping in and out of services to "get fed" without stopping to give, serve, and minister in the name of Jesus Christ. Pastors and church leaders have been wrong in the way that they have allowed people to become lukewarm.

We've been wrong when our preaching has held churchgoers to nominal accountability, as long as they understand the importance of the tithe.

We've been wrong in neglecting the follow-up of those who attend our mass meetings.

We've been wrong to substitute style for substance.

We've been wrong to focus on the way people dress instead of examining their inner lives and their hearts.

And we've been wrong in directing more ministry to foreign missions than into our own neighborhoods!

God isn't nearly as interested in numeric growth as He is in spiritual content. Big can be good as long as there's substance. And substance—biblical understanding, in-depth prayer, and spiritual growth—can only come through surrendered lives.

It is the flesh that inspires religious striving, and the enemy will push us to religious extremes and burnout if we're not burning inside with the oil of the Holy Ghost. That's why Jesus said in John 6:63, "It is the spirit that quickeneth; the flesh profiteth nothing: the words that I speak unto you, they are spirit, and they are life."

We are in the last day and the eleventh hour. We are in a revolutionary war. Those who have not radically surrendered to Jesus Christ will fall by the wayside, and Jesus will say, "I never knew you" (Matt. 7:23).

Now is the time and this is the hour to surrender to God's Word and receive a fresh infilling of the Holy Ghost! When surrender becomes a continual, radical lifestyle for the believer, the Holy Spirit will comfort, warn, direct, and protect the vision and plan of God's perfect will for our families and lives.

God is calling us to stay on His potter's wheel, surrender ourselves to His shaping, and represent Him with passion, integrity, and power before His return. With each passing moment, His return draws nearer. This is the last day, and then...eternity.

Recently, the nation of Israel celebrated her fifty-year Jubilee of restoration to her land. Other prophetic rumblings in America and around the world show that evil is eclipsing just as Jesus said it would before His return. The last day before eternity is just around the corner.

If you desire the Holy Spirit's power to ignite within you and carry you to the end, pray this prayer:

> *Father God, I come to You today in Jesus' name to ask Your for-giveness for my sin. I've allowed myself to get caught up in the everyday affairs of life to the point of rejecting Your Word and Spirit in my personal life. So today, Lord, I surrender all to You. I commit a time with You in prayer and Your Word. I exchange my goals for Your divine plan instead. I surrender my life completely to You, and I ask You to fill me with Your Holy Spirit to guide and empower me anew. I ask these things, in Jesus' name. Amen.*

It is the Spirit who gives life and trains us to become true wor-shipers on God's potter's wheel. Now we will discover how our Father, the Potter, wants to form us as time as we know it slips away toward eternity.

 **Two**

SHAPED ON THE
POTTER'S WHEEL

*Arise, and go down to the potter's house, and there I will cause
thee to hear my words. Then I went down to the potter's house,
and, behold, he wrought a work on the wheels.*

—JEREMIAH 18:2–3

Life sprints toward time's appointed finish line. The biological
stopwatch ticking within each of us unrelentingly winds down.
Less than a hundred years have usually transpired by the time we
come to the end of our days. In God's spectrum of eternity, this is a
few hours at best. So how we live and what we do while we are here
on earth really matters for eternity. The day before eternity will
soon pass by, and we will have an accounting to give.

Wherefore we labour, that, whether present or absent, we may
be accepted of him. For we must all appear before the judgment seat of Christ; that every one may receive the things
done in his body, according to that he hath done, whether it
be good or bad.

—2 CORINTHIANS 5:9–10

But too many of us trudge through life as strivers and doers out-side of God's rest, hoping that we can enter into the joy of our Master when this life ends. (See Matthew 25:21, 23.) This breaks my heart. I see precious saints every week who are performing min-istry in an attempt to earn God's approval in their spiritual quest.

I believe many Christians strive to "do things for God" because Law is so easy to understand. "Don't do this, and of course, absolutely do this, and you will earn this." There is no spiritual relationship in this kind of "doing" because performance instead of obedience is always at issue. Paul said if our works aren't birthed out of God's compassion and driving love, works are just works that profit us nothing.

> And though I bestow all my goods to feed the poor, and though I give my body to be burned, and have not charity, it profiteth me nothing.
>
> —1 CORINTHIANS 13:3

So, God has called us first and foremost to represent Him to the world as ambassadors of reconciliation. And we can only fully rep-resent Him through conforming to His image as a pliable piece of clay in the Potter's hands. When we strive in our own strength, we refuse the Holy Spirit's water that makes us pliable. As I said earlier, this is why Paul also wrote, "Nay but, O man, who art thou that repliest against God? Shall the thing formed say to him that formed it, Why hast thou made me thus?" (Rom. 9:20).

I've personally been through times when the tears streaming down my cheeks were so blinding and my mind was so blocked that I didn't know right from wrong. But I have always been able to pray through and remember the great promises of God's redemp-tion. Like Jeremiah, I've always been able to find my way back to the potter's house, rustle through the messy clay and cuttings that clutter the floor, and climb back up on my Master's wheel to hear His delivering words. And through it all, I've learned to trust Jesus.

Paul said, "For all things are for your sakes, that the abundant grace might through the thanksgiving of many redound to the glory of God" (2 Cor. 4:15).

"What do you mean, Paul?" we ask. "Do you mean your many beatings (five times with thirty-nine lashes, three times with rods), your three shipwrecks and stonings, your many sleepless nights, the cold and hunger you endured, and your many imprisonments were situations in life that God allowed you to go through in order that God might shape and form you?"

"Yes!" Paul would say to us.

They were all for his sake, because Paul knew where he came from and where he was going. That's why he wrote, "We having the same spirit of faith, according as it is written, I believed, and therefore have I spoken; we also believe, and therefore speak; knowing that he which raised up the Lord Jesus shall raise up us also by Jesus, and shall present us with you" (2 Cor. 4:13–14).

THE CHIEF OF SINNERS

Paul knew that he was the "chief" of sinners and that he was destined for eternity with Christ! He knew of Jesus' resurrection and that Jesus would raise him up in the age to come. So it didn't matter to Paul what obstacles lay in his path or what endurance it took to overcome them. Paul believed that any given day on his ministry calendar could be the last day before eternity, so he sought earnestly to make each day count.

The Christian doesn't rejoice because he's in prison just for the sake of rejoicing. When your thinking lines up with God's plan for your life, as Paul's thinking did, being in prison for Jesus' sake can turn out for good when life is lived on the Potter's wheel. Too often we want off the wheel just when God is about to shape and form us to receive His greatest blessing or calling for our lives.

Paul knew God was sovereign. On the way to Damascus to persecute and kill the church, a light blinded and saved him. Nothing Paul had done earned him the right to be chosen as an apostle. God is sovereign, and He chose Paul in mercy and grace. And Paul knew it.

Have you ever thought about what Paul was doing for those fourteen years after his conversion in the wilderness regions of Cyria and Cilicia that he mentions in Galatians? He was on the

Potter's wheel being transformed into the sovereign image of His Father from day to day and faith to faith.

THE POTTER'S WHEEL

The message of the Potter isn't comfortable. There are no soft couches or recliners on the Potter's wheel. While on His wheel, we feel the discomforting pressure of His hand forming us into His image. There we undergo God's loving quality control through the tempering and shaping of His message of severity and strength.

God always mixes His message of severity with compassion, mercy, and grace. Jesus was "wounded for our transgressions, he was bruised for our iniquities: the chastisement of our peace was upon him; and with his stripes we are healed" (Isa. 53:5). God is saying to us, "My Son was humiliated and suffered an agonizing death so that you can be delivered, eternally free."

For those stumbling into eternity, God says, "Climb up on My wheel." Once there, His message is always, "This is where you are...but this is where you need to be." He never leaves us in a quandary of wondering who, what, when, why, or where we need to be. The water of the Holy Spirit that makes us pliable allows each area of needed growth and formation to be reshaped in our loving Potter's hands. It is God who is in us to do exceedingly above anything we could ask according to His will and pleasure. And He will, as we yield to the Spirit's shaping on His turning wheel.

As time ticks away the eyes of God are looking to and fro throughout the earth for someone through whom He can show Himself strong. But so often He sees and hears us steeped in a gospel of humanism that rejects His forming message because it sounds too severe. Not many people who have reached the bottom will reject His offer of daily restoration. Once they have exhausted all their resources, when they can't lift their head off the canvas one more time, when their hands can't lift for another praise and their tongue is cleaving to the roof of their mouth, the Potter's wheel looks good—*if* they're serious about God's plan.

Prayer and study lubricate our Potter's wheel to allow His divine formation in our lives day to day. The Potter's house is a haven for the sweet surrendered who, like Paul, know where they came from and know where they're going. It's a place of repair and daily renewal: "For which cause we faint not; but though our outward man perish, yet the inward man is renewed day by day" (2 Cor. 4:16).

Today, more than ever, God is calling His church to be His modeling clay display. Paul says:

> For it is the God who commanded light to shine out of darkness, who has shone in our hearts to give the light of the knowledge of the glory of God in the face of Jesus Christ. But we have this treasure in earthen vessels, that the excellence of the power may be of God and not of us.
> —2 CORINTHIANS 4:6–7, NKJV

Therefore, Paul explains, because we have this ministry and have received His mercy, we faint not.

While you are on the Potter's wheel, He tells you where you are, where you're missing His will, and where you need to grow. He will also given you the supernatural ability to grow.

Do you understand? As pliable clay on the Potter's wheel, you are given the ability to see when you can't see, to hear what you can't hear, and to move when you can't move. "It is God which worketh in you both to will and to do of his good pleasure" (Phil. 2:13). "Christ in you, the hope of glory" (Col. 1:27).

Time is running out swiftly. So it is time for the American church and people to wake up from a gospel of humanism! I'm not ashamed to preach this every time the cameras turn on in my sanctuary, and now in the pages of this book. It's time we stopped lifting men so high that they fall so low, because the bigger we make them, the harder they fall. Every time a great church leader or politician disappoints us through human failure, we should have enough of Jesus within us to understand that clay is just dirt and sand until it is turned on the wheel by our Father's hand.

It's time to fix our eyes on our loving Potter again. It's time we stopped preaching and singing those songs that say, "I can do this, look at me! I am the seed of Abraham!" It's time we diverted our attention from what *we* are. No one should want to look at a dead corpse. That's the reason we put them in a grave. That's the reason we bury them. They stink! So does our dead flesh once we put it to death in our crucifixion with Christ. Take your eyes off yourself and others; fix them steadfastly on the Potter who shapes and forms you by the water of His Spirit and the knife of His Word.

PURPOSE! COMMISSION!

Purpose, commission, ability, and the anointing to give God the glory for our selfless ministry is what the Potter will instill in us when we stay positioned on His wheel. So it's time to shift our attention from the frailty of human flesh and lift our eyes to the One who turns the wheel. Help, strength, comfort, might, dominion, and authority are all in His hand, and He wants to form us "in Him" as His models throughout our culture.

None of us can do what we're required to do by God on our own. We can't hold our tongue without spewing polluted water here and there from time to time. We can't stay out of the devil's traps by ourselves. We can't fight the demonic forces of the darkened regions of the underworld on our own. Outside of God's powerful incarnation, we have many inabilities. But I believe the greatest inability the church has experienced has been the inability to perceive that without God's anointing, we can do nothing.

Haddon Spurgeon wrote, "Apart from the Spirit of God, we can do nothing. We are as ships without the wind in our sails. We are chariots without steeds to pull them. As branches without sap, we are withered. Apart from the Spirit of God, we can do nothing."[1] And he was right!

Today we hear so much about our Christian rights that we sound like the devil himself: "I have a right, and I have a will . . ." Remember Satan's words in Isaiah 14:14: "*I will* ascend above the heights of the clouds; *I will* be like the most High" (emphasis added).

In this last day, it's time to start saying to God, "I will climb up on Your potter's wheel, Father. I will humble myself as a lump of clay in Your hands to allow You to form me as a model of Your integrity." Then once you've acknowledged that, climb up, sit down, shut up, and let your Father go to work.

When you know where you're headed and where you've been, you can understand the reason why Satan fights so hard to keep you unwilling and off God's wheel. The devil didn't beat up Paul and try to kill him because of who he was. Remember, Saul of Tarsus was one of Satan's closest collaborators in his "respectable" Pharisee days. Saul was one of his best workers who, like other false religionists, was working his way to hell. So once Saul had been aborted out of his former master's grip on the road to Damascus, the reason why Satan opposed him so tirelessly night and day wasn't because of who Paul *was*. He did it because of who suddenly Paul *was not*.

Suddenly, one day Saul was converted and his earthen vessel that Satan had used through dead works was filled with the presence of God. The reason you keep the devil up nights walking the floors and dialing 9-1-1 is because of who is living within you. He who is living within you is greater than he who is in the world. The Holy Spirit's treasure indwells your earthen vessel. So Satan attacks you because of that treasure deposited in you. He desires to still the Holy Ghost's ability and enabling so that you will be a powerless saint.

Satan knows he can hinder you if he can block the treasure. So he does what he can to deceive and delude so that you will become hardened and resistive to the Potter's water of the Spirit. If you are hardened, you will stay off the Potter's wheel. Whenever you are off His wheel, you remove yourself from His loving control, which is forming and shaping you.

That's why Paul could say in authority that all things were for his sake:

> But we have this treasure in earthen vessels, that the excellency of the power may be of God, and not of us. We are troubled on every side, yet not distressed; we are perplexed, but not in despair; persecuted, but not forsaken; cast down, but not destroyed; always bearing about in the body the dying of the Lord Jesus, that the life also of Jesus might be made manifest in our body.
>
> —2 CORINTHIANS 4:7–10

Paul couldn't make this statement if his many exploits were undertaken on his own. So often we feel when we're distressed that we must act or react to take the pressure off. So we quit; we run. We deny; we leave. We do anything but cleave.

Right in the middle of circumstances that are shaping us, when we feel the imprint of the Father's molding hands, just as Sarai did, we will be tempted to offer Hagar to Abram and birth an Ishmael who continues to burden and wear down our integrity and calling. Whenever you are off the Potter's wheel, you will birth an Ishmael. We sense the wheel spinning and feel the pressure of the Potter's hands. When we forget our mission and purpose and refuse His touch, in that moment we birth an Ishmael.

LET GO OF THE POTTER'S WHEEL

God in His sovereignty has already foreseen every obstacle you will face. He has made a way of escape—through growth—to see you completely through. So quit taking your situations into your own hands to form and mold yourself. Learn the art of sweet surrender. Make the wheel your way of life. As the old song goes, "Have Thine own way, Lord! Have Thine own way! Thou art the potter, I am the clay."[2] The letter of the do's and don'ts of the law kills, but the Spirit of God gives life.

The surrendered don't faint, not because we are trying not to faint. We aren't trying to avoid anything. We're submitting to win in the confidence that, come hell or high water, we will never faint. Every time we praise the Lord, the Holy Spirit rises up and takes us to another level of blessing as God puts us on His potter's wheel and crushes us to death.

> For we which live are always delivered unto death for Jesus' sake, that the life also of Jesus might be made manifest in our mortal flesh. So then death worketh in us, but life in you.
> —2 CORINTHIANS 4:11–12

Make this your prayer: "Here's my life, Lord! Here's the frailty of my human flesh. Here I am as filthy rags, poured out like a drink offering and broken bread. Here I am climbing up on Your potter's wheel again. Lord, take my life and make it be consecrated to You!"

Surrendered Christians understand the price and inner work that happen whenever we're asked to make a payment: "For which cause we faint not; but though our outward man perish, yet the inward man is renewed day by day. For our light affliction, which is but for a moment, worketh for us a far more exceeding and eternal weight of glory" (2 Cor. 4:16–17).

SCOT-FREE GRACE?

We get away with so much in our current dispensation of unconditional love. Things Old Testament worshipers would have been stoned for we get away with now, seemingly scot-free. At least we think we do. But the price is paid, and consequences are felt through the heavy burdens so many Christians are carrying in our modern age.

So many of us get caught up in busyness just to make ends meet. We catch a church service on the run, then we're off again to make ends meet again. There's no purpose in this. Jesus called this the lifestyle of the Gentiles who are totally consumed with where they will live and what they will eat. There is no place for God in their lives.

THREE POTTER'S MESSAGES

The Potter's house is a place of safety as well as retreat. There are three lessons to be learned by those who go there.

1. THE FIRST LESSON OF THE POTTER'S HOUSE IS SOVEREIGNTY.

The Potter has absolute authority over the clay, and there's nothing the clay can do about it.

You say, "But wait a minute. Natural potter's clay doesn't have a will, but I do."

"Oh, really?" I say. "Well then, who gave you your will? God did. And if you've really called Jesus 'Lord' in an attitude of surrender, God's will should be the only thing that matters in life. If

Jesus is Lord, then Jesus is king, and His plan and vision should be everything."

Remember Paul's admonition, "Who art thou that repliest against God? Shall the thing formed say to him that formed it, Why hast thou made me thus?" (Rom. 9:20).

2. GOD USES LIFE'S CIRCUMSTANCES (REPRESENTED BY THE WHEEL) TO HELP FORM OUR LIVES.

Without the potter's wheel, there can be no formation of the clay. So God's wheel turns amid our circumstances as we allow His involvement in our lives every day.

3. THE POTTER SOFTENS AND SHAPES THE CLAY OF OUR LIVES THROUGH THE WATER OF HIS SPIRIT.

The third message of the Potter's house is us—the Potter's clay. As we remain pliable and soft with the Holy Spirit's water, God will form us in our circumstances.

So God is the Potter. We are the clay. The wheel is life's circumstances that happen every day. And I'm not just talking about negative circumstances. The Potter wants you to learn how to give Him all the glory when things are going right! So He wants you turning on His formative wheel when you are on the mountaintop as well as in the valley, because He is everywhere; He knows where He wants you to be.

CIRCUMSTANCES ARE TEMPORARY; GLORY IS FOREVER

This is where Paul's "all things are for our sakes" message should really hit home. Paul believed the time had been shortened in his century (1 Cor. 7:29) and that Jesus could return any day. He understood his purpose. Paul also knew his circumstances were only temporary, and he had his mind fully fixed on the things above (Col. 3:1). Circumstances were no reason to cancel ministry trips. Jail cells were places to rejoice, to write letters, and to win his guards to the Lord. Paul knew his circumstances were merely the wheels on which the Potter formed his life.

> While we look not at the things which are seen, but at the
> things which are not seen: for the things which are seen are
> temporal; but the things which are not seen are eternal.
> —2 CORINTHIANS 4:18

This is where we as the church must come to terms with our daily affairs if our lives are to ever become vessels for noble use. Don't misunderstand me. Many of us have taken our seat on God's character-forming wheel. But many more are still running around from this circumstance to another one in a blur of activity in anxiety and stress. Every time Paul ran out of himself, the Holy Ghost filled him to overflowing.

Grace upon grace is what the Father works into our lives through His Holy Spirit's power when we reject the world's rat race and climb up on God's wheel.

SAY AGAIN AND AGAIN—GOD IS SOVEREIGN!

God is sovereign, and He has a purpose for you that must be fulfilled. But He can't do it until you're formed enough to represent Him. The last thing He wants for your life is another broken potsherd littering the Potter's field.

You may think, *That wheel is going to crush me! I'm never going to get off of here. I'm off balance! I'm dizzy! I'm quitting! I'm running!* These are the kinds of sounds hardened pots make before they break. Hardened pots can't see beyond the temporal circumstances of a trial. And they can't grow in grace when the pressure is off—because they're too busy doing *nothing* within the will of God. Busyness consumes them with doing what they will, not what God wills.

Read how Jesus describes doing His will and not your own:

> I am the vine, ye are the branches: he that abideth in me, and
> I in him, the same bringeth forth much fruit: for without me
> ye can do nothing.
> —JOHN 15:5

So, we need to partner with God's sovereignty in every thing. Every step we take in time must first be projected onto God's eternal screen: "While we look not at the things which are seen, but at the things which are not seen: for the things which are seen are temporal; but the things which are not seen are eternal" (2 Cor. 4:18).

Remember this: The Holy Spirit has been where you can't go. He dwells in the inner courts of God's redeeming wisdom and knows what you need to overcome in life's trials, tests, and temptations every day. He will remind you to stay humble. And He will remind you to be bold. The Potter's wheels are just instruments that eventually stop.

What you must understand is this: Whatever you're going through will either refine you or destroy you; it will bend you or break you. If you resist God's sovereign grace, His wheel becomes loving discipline. But if you embrace sweet surrender, His wheel becomes the forming place for you to develop perseverance and strength. God is more concerned for your response than for your circumstance. Fix your eyes on the Potter, not on the wheel.

GOD'S PLACE OF FORMATION

Jesus is the Potter! He will form and reform you to pass His quality control. It was Jesus who allowed Himself to become flesh like us and to be tempted like us, so our Heavenly Father could relate to us.

When Adam sinned, death set in, and his original being was deformed. Since Adam, we all need reforming. The Potter formed Adam from the dust of the ground. Then He breathed into him the breath of life. But he died and was deformed from God's original intention. But when Jesus appeared to the disciples behind those closed doors in John 20:19, God breathed back into man the life that Adam had forfeited. "And when he had said this, he breathed on them, and saith unto them, Receive ye the Holy Ghost" (John 20:22).

When we're born again our inner man is re-created, so there's nothing else needed to perfect that until the trump blows and we receive our new glorified bodies. But our outer man is in continual need of reformation. You just stop watching what you're eating, and before you know it, your body will deform. And unless you reform your eating habits you'll deform into a blimp.

The same is true of your thinking. You just keep those pathetic worldly images and ideas that polluted television's airwaves pour into your mind, and your mind will deform into a paranoid mess of immorality, hype, and fear. The Potter renews your mind, giving you the mind of Christ.

God's Place of Reformation

The Potter's wheel is not only a place of *formation;* it is also a place of *reformation.* Every time you stop to pray and consult God's Word, you put yourself up on His wheel to report for formation or reformation that day. Jeremiah acknowledged this process when he said, "And the vessel that he made of clay was marred in the hand of the potter: so he made it again another vessel, as seemed good to the potter to make it" (Jer. 18:4).

But Old Testament Jeremiah could only acknowledge our clay. New Testament Paul, on the other hand, could acknowledge the presence of the Holy Spirit who, under our New Covenant, now dwells within.

> For God, who commanded the light to shine out of darkness, hath shined in our hearts, to give the light of the knowledge of the glory of God in the face of Jesus Christ. But we have this treasure in earthen vessels, that the excellency of the power may be of God, and not of us.
>
> —2 Corinthians 4:6–7

"I'll make a new vessel. I'll fix this thing up. I'm going to form it and give it purpose, and the very gates of hell won't be able to prevail against it," the Father said.

But the vessel can't do it on its own because outside of Christ, we're only clay.

All things are for our sakes when we're walking the path of God's will. Human beings are frail creatures, but if we submit ourselves to the obedience of death, the Holy Spirit will resurrect us! When the church grasps the revelation of "Christ in us, the hope of glory," we will trample down the brazen gates of hell!

As the day before eternity passes, we will laugh in the face of temptation! We'll rejoice in the midst of tribulation, because we will hear those wheels turning us into powerful vessels of End-Time harvest. Like Paul, we'll get up when we're knocked down and brush ourselves off to move on to the next town. If prison awaits us, we'll turn it into a cathedral of praise, because greater is He that's in us than he that is in the world!

So get on the wheel to find your purpose. Get hooked up with God's sovereign plan, and let the wheel of life form and reform you in our loving Potter's hands. You can't get yourself into victory any more than you can make yourself pregnant. If you're going to walk in the miraculous that these last days will require, you're going to have to be like Mary. You will have to be overshadowed by the Holy Ghost.

It's the last day before eternity, and you are being shaped by the Potter's hand. The day does not shape you nor does the passing of time. The events of the day cannot change you. Only the Potter shapes and changes you. And in His hands, you will not just survive this last day and its final hours; you will overcome!

_____

_____

_____

_____

_____

_____

_____

_____

_____

_____

_____

_____

_____

_____

_____

_____

_____

_____

_____

_____

 **THREE**

CROSSING
THE VICTOR'S LINE

*But he that shall endure unto the end, the same shall be saved.
And this gospel of the kingdom shall be preached in all the world
for a witness unto all nations; and then shall the end come.*
— MATTHEW 24:13–14

*For which cause we faint not; but though our outward man
perish, yet the inward man is renewed day by day.*
— 2 CORINTHIANS 4:16

In this day before eternity, the revolutionary church of Jesus Christ has just one mission statement: *Preach the gospel to the ends of the earth for a witness to all nations.*

In this day before eternity, the saints in Christ's bride must achieve one goal for the mission to be accomplished: *Endure to the end.* In other words, you and I are called to finish the race, complete the course, and cross the victor's line. The race doesn't go to the polished, the educated, the proud, the self-righteous, or the religious. It doesn't go to the fleet, fast, swift, or blinding-speed starters that leave the field behind in the first twenty-five meters. The winners of this race to eternity are all those who finish...so finish strong!

ONLY THOSE CHANGED WILL ENDURE

God accepts us where we are and loves us too much to leave us there. Once you join this army marching into eternal glory, you will never be the same again. Once you march with this army, the world around you—your family, colleagues, teammates, and schoolmates—will never be the same again.

Following Jesus, our Commander in Chief, will change your life. Heeding His call to "follow Me" means that you will be eternally changed—a new creation in Him (2 Cor. 3:17).

Some join a revolutionary movement because they are bored and are looking for their circumstances and situations to change. Revolutionary movements are conspicuous vehicles of change. But the change effected by Christ is unlike any other revolution in history.

The Reformation revolution sought ecclesiastical change.
The American Revolution sought democratic change.
The French Revolution sought political change.
The Marxist revolution sought economic change.
The Nazi revolution sought ethnic change.
The Civil Rights revolution sought social change.

But the Jesus revolution does not foster cultural or societal change on any external level though every aspect of life is radically changed by the gospel. All other revolutions provoke change from the outside in, but Christ revolutionizes life from the inside out.

A revolutionary church marching into eternity's glory wins battles one heart at a time. God's intent is that the church be a vehicle of change, and in order to change the world, those in the church must first themselves be changed by the radical, regenerating power of the Holy Spirit poured out by God through Christ as He reconciles persons to Himself.

God never intended for the church to be an institution that we join. It is a revolutionary movement that offers people the opportunity to change...forever! If the church were a club, you could join it. If it were an organization, you could be hired. If it were a group of mercenaries, you could enlist. If it were a team, you could try out.

But the church is a family. The only way to enter a family is to be born into it. Jesus said that you must be born again—born of water and the Spirit—in order to become part of His revolutionary movement (John 3).

There is no way in the world to resist the revolutionary movement of Christ called the *ecclesia*. The murderous, religious leader Saul tried to stop this revolution in the first century A.D. He arrested, persecuted, libeled, stoned, murdered, and drove out followers of Jesus wherever he could find them. But what happened to Saul is a lesson in how persons changed by Christ, born into the family of God, and swept up in the revolutionary movement of the church become the overcoming change agents that turn the world upside down and that endure to the end.

SAUL: CHANGED INTO PAUL, GOD'S VEHICLE OF CHANGE

The Jewish leaders in Damascus were divided over the religious developments arising from that nerve-racking week that Saul had been saved. The Pharisee's sudden conversion to the sect he had been zealously persecuting and murdering just days earlier was confounding many and converting more. Finally, the Jews resolved to take his life. This was their only recourse. The testimonies and miracles surrounding their fallen one's new cause had not been countered by the religious authorities. So a plot was conceived. Assassins watched the city's gates day and night.

"Lowered down over the wall in a basket you say? What manner of travel is this for one such as myself? If death be God's will, then so be it!" argued the new convert at hearing the news.

"They mean to murder you, Saul!" Ananias pleaded. "Please! We have everything in order. We should not tempt the Lord at this time, man of God! There are fifty men hungry for the honor of destroying your heresies, shedding your blood, and collecting the silver offered for your life!"

"As you say then, brother. I will go. But where?" Saul asked.

"We have informed our brethren in Jerusalem of your salvation. They are expecting you within two days," Ananias comforted his new friend.

This is probably how Saul's conversation sounded during those first zealous weeks of his miraculous conversion. This former persecutor of the church was finally experiencing the Holy Spirit's grace in his life, and nothing else mattered except his ministry course. This was a new day for Saul, renamed Paul. In fact, it was Paul's day before eternity.

As the days pushed on in this humble vessel's ministry, Paul would be shaped by God through many battles into the man who would represent God to the nations of Gentiles, lost and hungering for a revelation of the true God. Without his epistles, the church would still be ignorant of who God really is and what He wants us to be today.

There is a battle being waged today in the culture mills of America over the destiny of men's souls. As the day before eternity draws near, there will be a winnowing, a separation of those things in the lives of God's people that have kept them off the Potter's wheel and bound them as slaves of the secular state.

As the Spirit called Saul from out of his murdering rage against followers of Jesus, so He is calling the church: "Climb up on My wheel of character development." Thousands upon thousands are responding in this final hour. Many are shouldering the Spirit's call to demonstrate Christ. They are being shaped—as Paul was—in the battle of humble service into bold, loving saints.

This remnant organization of the Holy Ghost in the church today is venturing beyond the hype and humanism of so much modern preaching to seek out God's best in every area of life. They are placing themselves upon the Potter's wheel every day and inviting the gray areas in their lives to be exposed by the Holy Ghost's burning presence. They are stopping to pray and consult God's Word. They are being shaped and formed into Christ's image on the Potter's wheel.

How about you? Will you join this ragtag army that is being forged in the fires of godly service? Will you lay down your life to give God the glory today? Tomorrow is too late!

God is inspiring those with ears to hear as time slips away. God's Spirit is challenging us to be more, do more, learn more, and grow more. He is transitioning His people away from the milksop, milktoast institution we've called the church into a remnant of overcomers who will do mighty exploits in their homes, in the church, and on the job.

Our heavenly Father is no respecter of persons (Acts 10:34), so what He did for Saul, He will do for you. God is sovereign. But I have a notion that if the church wasn't praying about their horrible situation, God might not have blinded their nemesis, Saul, and stopped him in his tracks. There was a remnant of saints praying for those who persecuted them because Jesus had commanded them to pray for and love their enemies (Matt. 5:44). God answered their prayers. Saul was aborted from hell's designs and birthed into God's loving care. God sent him on a mission that would eventually touch you and me with the Good News of Jesus Christ.

Enduring in the face of opposition, regardless of the stakes, is a blatant invitation the Holy Ghost never resists. It is the spiritual environment in which God forms noble women and men.

"All right, Ananias, I get your point. But where do I go now?" Saul probably asked.

"On to more lessons of Christian humility, Paul, but you must be alive to learn them. I sense the Spirit's warning," Ananias probably said.

DON'T QUIT! NEVER GIVE UP!

Quitting is never an option for those enduring to the end. Paul knew he couldn't quit. In his early conversion zeal, he probably lacked needed wisdom. Wisdom grows out of applied knowledge. Paul was applying his new knowledge in Damascus, proving that Jesus was the Christ (Acts 9:20). From there he traveled to Jerusalem, then to the regions of Syria and Cilicia, and eventually into the world of his day to establish the church of Jesus Christ.

What if Paul had quit in Damascus? What if he had shrunk back from his new opposition and decided to blend in with the other

Christians of his day? What if he had chosen to do what so many of us do today in the church? So many run at the first hint of battle.

When the unlovely smear us, we smear back.

When the world system says, "You can't do that," we cower back.

When the mission gets long, we want a vacation.

When the money runs out, we find a foxhole and hide instead of going forward in prayer and into the battle.

THE BATTLE IS FOUGHT
IN TRENCHES THAT BRIDGE ETERNITY

He that endures to the end is the one who will be saved. When all hell broke loose against Paul in his many battles, he sought the Lord's relief, and for his many troubles, the Lord dispensed His grace: "For this thing I besought the Lord thrice, that it might depart from me. And he said unto me, My grace is sufficient for thee: for my strength is made perfect in weakness. Most gladly therefore will I rather glory in my infirmities, that the power of Christ may rest upon me" (2 Cor. 12:8–9).

Grace is "the operational power of God that sets the believer free." But it must be requisitioned (asked for!) in the trenches that bridge eternity.

Some people give aspirin more time to work than God. When the going gets tough, they take an aspirin and bow out of the conflict. But there are vast numbers of other men and women whose destiny should have been sealed by defeat and discouragement. However, they astounded their adversaries as they stood undaunted in the crucible of conflict.

What the enemy has designed to cause these remnant warriors' ultimate demise, they endure and overcome. These are those who avail themselves in the Potter's house as gold and silver vessels of noble use and honor. The Bible declares, "But in a great house there are not only vessels of gold and of silver, but also of wood and of earth; and some to honour, and some to dishonour" (2 Tim. 2:20).

Mighty vessels of God aren't born that way. They are built in battle, forged in the face of opposition, and finished in the kiln of the Potter's fire as rock-solid examples of God's unfailing love. Of such, Dr. Martin Luther King, Jr. said, "The ultimate measure of a man is not where he stands in moments of comfort and convenience but where he stands at times of challenge and controversy."[1]

Before he had been finished in the fire, the apostle Peter warmed himself by the world's fire and denied his Lord three times before the cock crowed in the morning. Then that same Peter stood with fearless tenacity on the day of Pentecost and preached a powerful message that brought three thousand men to the Lord. This former fisherman had originally checked out, took two aspirin, and rented a video. But because he was open, honest, and pliable, the Lord quickly launched him back into battle once he received new bearings on the Potter's wheel.

God used Paul's stoning, shipwreck, snakebite, and beatings to build him into the apostle of love who could confront the world in boldness and at the same time pen 1 Corinthians 13:

> Charity suffereth long, and is kind; charity envieth not; charity vaunteth not itself, is not puffed up, doth not behave itself unseemly, seeketh not her own, is not easily provoked, thinketh no evil.
>
> —vv. 4–5

Read in church history how Christ's beloved apostle John was boiled in oil. Then read his Gospel, three epistles, and finally, the revelation he received from Christ because of his endurance when banished on Patmos, the Roman Empire's Alcatraz of that day: "He that saith he is in the light, and hateth his brother, is in darkness even until now" (1 John 2:9).

Peter prayed for ten days and preached for ten minutes and three thousand men were saved. Today, we preach for ten hours and pray for ten minutes—no wonder we give up along the way. We strive and work, then get distracted by this or that. But the one who endures will triumph in the end.

Stranded in the snows of Valley Forge, George Washington and his soldiers endured great agony in order to birth the United States. He fought the cold. He fought the pain. The outcome to the great general was greater than the comforts surrender could have offered in reducing the pain.

Ludwig van Beethoven went deaf. From his seventh symphony on, this man wrote without the physical ability to hear.

Raised in abject poverty, Abraham Lincoln overcame his humble beginnings by reading everything he could find, and he rose through the ranks to become America's greatest president. If he would have succumbed to the failure of losing many elections before running for the presidency, Lincoln would have stayed a country lawyer, just working to make ends meet.

In the twentieth century, Glenn Cunningham was told by the doctors that he would never walk again, but he went on to run the mile and break the world record in 1934.

Albert Einstein was diagnosed with Asberger Syndrome, the same as my little boy. They said Einstein would never learn, go to school, ride a bike, or play with other children because he was unteachable and retarded. They said the same thing about my son. But I wouldn't listen.

Dr. Martin Luther King, Jr. stood undaunted in the face of a bigoted America that daily provoked and tempted him to quit. Like Paul, when he was thrown into jail, he wrote and prayed. Read his "Letter From a Birmingham Jail" sometime and see if you don't see the epistle of the Civil Rights movement written by this great man while he was unjustly incarcerated.

Have you ever had a Coke? In their first twelve months of business, Coca-Cola only sold four hundred. If they would have been deterred, there would never have been a Coke float!

Wayne Gretzky, unarguably the greatest hockey player that ever set foot on a rink, was told when he tried out for the pros that he was fifty pounds too light.

Michael Jordan, unarguably the greatest basketball player to ever set foot on a court, was cut by the coach from his high school basketball team. But he refused to quit. I love that commercial where Michael says, "The ball has been placed in my hands with less than ten seconds to go for the winning shot a number of times, and eighty-four of them I've missed. I've missed more shots in my career than I've made. I've lost thousands of games in my career."

If Jordan allowed crowd and press pressures to keep him down and out, he would never have rebounded the way he has as basketball's Babe Ruth of all time.

Dr. Seuss submitted his first book, *And to Think I Saw It on Mulberry Street,* to twenty-six publishers, with twenty-six rejections for his efforts. But the twenty-seventh publisher accepted it, and the rest is literature history. Millions of Seuss books have been printed since then because Dr. Seuss wouldn't say quit.

Every one of these outstanding examples of endurance could have shrunk in the face of adversity and drifted off into obscurity. But they didn't. The opposition they encountered in their battles served to build them instead of making them casualties of war.[2]

We are all clay in this life, and if sheer will power allows for the tenacity of success in the lives who don't serve God's plan, how much more so does the Holy Ghost's conforming of those whom God is calling to become like Christ.

I'm tired of these shooting-star preachers who are plastered all over the magazines and television screens of America. During their "season" you can find them running from this meeting to that one. But in a few years' time, you can't find them. Why? When the devil pulls out his heavy artillery on them, and he does especially to God's servants who are so visible, they run for cover instead of running into prayer. They go AWOL and then desert. They have no understanding of Paul's truth that we discussed in the previous chapter, the "all things are for your sake" statement. They refuse God's building process that can only come in the heat of battle.

It happens to the anonymous Christian, too. Let me paraphrase something that A. W. Tozer said: The average Christian is a harmless enough thing. The devil couldn't care less whether you go to Sunday school today when he knows you're going to quit tomorrow. He doesn't care how much you pray today when he knows the thing he's been planning for forty-five years is going to show up on your doorstep tomorrow. He's confident that when you see it, you'll give up the race and quit.

Satan has succeeded in weakening our resolution, neutralizing our convictions, and taming our urges to do exploits. In many pockets of Christianity we've become little more than sad statistics that contribute financially to the upkeep of a religious institution.

Compromise is the language of the devil! Compromise takes the pressure off and makes you feel better when you quit. But it will take you out of the race, and eventually out of the stadium, because Satan will always give you just the right words to justify your actions and to take you deeper into sin.[3]

ENDURANCE: THE AIM OF ALL SPIRITUAL ATTACKS

Endurance is the aim of all spiritual attacks, because if Satan can stop forward motion, then he can stop the one he blocks from fulfilling God's plan for his life. Remember that God doesn't need you to accomplish His plan. God will implement His plan with or without you. So if you quit, God will simply find someone else who is a yielded and willing vessel.

So get up! Don't quit! You may have been told your skin is the wrong color. You may have believed the lie that you don't have enough education, good looks, ability, or credentials. Don't listen to the father of lies! Jesus spoke of those who believe the lies of the devil, "Ye are of your father the devil, and the lusts of your father ye will do. He was a murderer from the beginning, and abode not in the truth, because there is no truth in him. When he speaketh a lie, he speaketh of his own: for he is a liar, and the father of it" (John 8:44). This is Satan's only weapon. He can only attack through the tool of deception. But if you believe it, his deception will become your reality; you'll quit with excuses that twist your actions to prove it was God's will. Perhaps one of these excuses fits you:

- "Well, yes, pastor, I know my ministry was growing, but when the finances dwindled and the city's favor left, I recognized it was God saying that it was time to move on."

- "My marriage was growing as I deferred my rights to accept and forgive anything that happened in the home. But that last incident was the straw that broke the camel's back. He knew I wouldn't stand for that."

- "I finally realized those critics would never change, so I tendered my resignation and moved on for the next two years at my next assigned church."

Stop making excuses. You don't have to quit. You don't have to give up. You can hope beyond hope, like Abraham, being fully assured that what God promised, He will also bring to pass. "Who [Abraham] against hope believed in hope, that he might become the father of many nations, according to that which was spoken, So shall thy seed be" (Rom. 4:18). Abraham made mistakes, just like Paul. But he didn't pack it in and return to Haran when the seed that would make him a great nation didn't show up the first year he left. Twenty-five years would pass before God brought it about. You can stand up to the forge of the battle and let God put in you what you need at that moment to see the situation through.

It's important for you to stop and pray. Spend time with God every day! When you do, He will take the wheels of life's situations and give you the opportunity to prove His wisdom.

The most important time to lift your hands in praise is when they're weighted down with difficulties and trials. This is the time to reach up and get on the Potter's wheel and let Him shape and form you. The race is not to the swift, but to the one who stands fearlessly in the face of defeat. When you seek God earnestly in prayer and study, He will show you why your problem came about, give you the solution to walk through it, and then build in you the resources to overcome again.

Heaven's rewards are reserved for those who refuse to be denied their crown of righteousness. They are reserved for those who more than anything else look forward to saying one day, "I have fought a good fight, I have finished my course, I have kept the faith: Henceforth there is laid up for me a crown of righteousness, which the Lord, the righteous judge, shall give me at that day: and not to me only, but unto all them also that love his appearing" (2 Tim. 4:7–8).

Those who surrender in battle forget they are hooked up to an irresistible power. They have forgotten the words of their Master: "Ye shall receive power after that the Holy Ghost is come upon you" (Acts 1:8). They dialogue with the devil. Like Eve, instead of withstanding his perverted misstatements of truth, they entertain his ideas and rationalize themselves right under his control. This is why Jesus said, "I beheld Satan as lightning fall from heaven. Behold, I give unto you power to tread on serpents and scorpions, and over all the power of the enemy: and nothing shall by any means hurt you" (Luke 10:18–19).

Peter wrote, "Be sober, be vigilant; because your adversary the devil, as a roaring lion, walketh about, seeking whom he may devour: whom resist stedfast in the faith, knowing that the same afflictions are accomplished in your brethren that are in the world" (1 Pet. 5:8–9).

In This Final Day, Resist the Devil

It is the day before eternity. In this final hour, the devil has pulled out all the stops in trying to defeat us. He tempts us at every turn to quit. He accuses us with past sins and failures. But we have the power to overcome the enemy.

We must confront and resist the devil. Jesus has given us grace to overcome his evil power. But somewhere along the line many of us have forgotten that greater is He who is in us, than he who is in the world (1 John 4:4). Somehow we have forgotten that we have in our possession the sword of the Spirit—God's absolute and unfailing Word. Somehow we fix our eyes on the circumstances of life instead of fixing our eyes on the author and finisher of our faith (Heb. 12:2). Sadly we resist the Potter's wheel and find ourselves being crushed under the wheels of Satan's chariots of destruction.

So what if Satan wants to sift you? God will refine you in the process and have you smarter and quicker the next time around. Peter was built in his battle because Jesus warned him of this exact request: "Simon, Simon, behold, Satan hath desired to have you, that he may sift you as wheat: but I have prayed for thee, that thy faith fail not: and when thou art converted, strengthen thy brethren" (Luke 22:31–32).

The actual translation of this passage shows that Satan requisitioned and received permission to come against Peter. And Peter was down for a while. He fell prey to the spirit of fear and briefly denied he even knew Jesus.

Peter was down, but not out. He was confused, but undeterred. When Mary's words proclaiming their Lord's resurrection hit his ears, he was the first to race into His empty tomb. He was the first to grace the upper room. And he was also the first to embrace the Gentiles at the Roman Cornelius's home.

Peter's battles built him. Look at his before-and-after picture. Look at him in the Gospels as he represents us all in his boisterous prideful air. Then read his two epistles. If God could build Peter in battle into the example he became, He can certainly shape and build us in the battle.

God is building in battle a last days' military force the like of which history has never seen. Our weapons are not carnal, but they are mighty for the tearing down of Satan's strongholds of deception and intrigue (2 Cor. 10:14). Our uniforms are the pure white gowns of righteousness unsoiled by human compromise or might.

Yes, we may fail, but we get up and move forward.

Yes, we may be tempted, but we overcome by the word of our testimony and the blood of the Lamb (Rev. 12:11). As the last day before eternity draws near, God is raising up an army that is raising His standard in battle. Our burning desire in life is the gospel of Jesus Christ. We want to preach, teach, and breathe the gospel in order to see the manifestation of the sons of God in the earth.

Since you are reading this book, I believe this is your desire. The time of the status quo is over, and you know it. We've lived in a society where right has been wrong for so long that righteousness has become the abnormal thing. Isaiah said, "Woe to those who call evil good, and good evil" (Isa. 5:20, NKJV). There has never been an American generation more willing to fulfill his words. So God is calling His remnant church to stand up in our generation and be willing to take the devil's best shot.

God rebuked the church in Thyatira for compromising with the woman Jezebel, who represented the world's ungodly, quitting ways. But at the same time He commended Thyatira's remnant church for resisting the deep things of Satan. I believe this is where we are in the church today. (See Revelation 2:18–24.)

Satan has an inner circle of darkened hearts to whom he has imparted the mystery of iniquity in the depths of degradation. These doctors of damnation have worked like leaven permeating the mind-set of the body of Christ to the point that even many of us today are calling evil good. "Quit! Stop! Don't get involved!" these cultural voices blare out constantly. We must be careful not to produce sins of omission—those offers of grace and kindness to others that God has commanded us to enact. White becomes gray. Then, sins of commission begin to take place: "After all, everyone does it" is the compromising invitation of these evil workers today in the church.

> Like a muddied spring or a polluted well is a righteous man
> who gives way to the wicked.
> —PROVERBS 25:26, NIV

The wicked say, "Stop; go no farther with God. You'll be sorry, so give yourself a break." But God is calling His own into the fray to prevail within the testing—to overcome and prove their faith.

IT'S THE FINAL HOUR; TIME IS SHORT

Time is short. Remember, James said it is a vapor that appears and disappears in a short amount of time. So he says, "For that ye ought to say, If the Lord will, we shall live, and do this, or that" (James 4:15). Listen to what the Lord is saying to His remnant church today: "Cower not at the battle in your challenged home life! You have listened to the voice of the world that says you have a right to quit. But I say that I hate divorce! Love, forgive, humble, seek counsel, overcome, grow, and give!

"Love and submit to the unlovely you know; represent Me in righteousness. Don't repay evil for evil; I will help you turn the other cheek.

"Present yourselves as vessels ready to do My will. Start small, grow big, and I will turn the wheel!

"Pick up your cross and follow Me! Follow My path to Calvary! I will never leave or forsake you! I will build you in battle with power and love. Don't stop; move forward. Don't allow My sacrifice to be in vain!"

Number yourself among God's built-in battle remnant who move through life undaunted by the challenges that line life's paths. When criticism snaps your head back with a right upper cut, counter with a swift left. Hit the floor in the Potter's house and receive God's good grace to restore your course. Resist the devil who prowls about as a roaring lion, "seeking"—notice, not "destroying"—but "seeking whom he may devour." For every lie of Satan there are a hundred verses of truth. For every setback in business, there is a comeback in wisdom truth that could only have been gained in the middle of that storm.

You are being built in battle during this last day and final hour. Stand firm. Stay on the Potter's wheel and invite Christ to complete His good work in you!

Why is it so important that you stand firm and endure to the end? If you quit now, someone who needs a radical change in life through your witness will be lost. A future child, grandchild, or great-grandchild is depending on you to finish the race. Your church, Sunday school class, choir, mission team, or evangelism team is counting on you to finish the race. Someone who desperately needs to be born into this revolutionary movement of Christ will experience His life-changing, saving power and grace *because you endure to the end.*

Those who need Jesus to change them are depending on you to preach the gospel, feed their starving lips, proclaim healing in the name of Jesus, or speak deliverance to their tormented souls. Many will be lost if you quit. Endure to the end. Stand firm. Finish strong and be God's change agent in this last day before eternity.

_____

_____

_____

_____

_____

_____

_____

_____

_____

_____

_____

_____

_____

_____

_____

_____

_____

_____

_____

_____

 **Four**

A COMMITTED, IMMOVABLE HEART

Simon, Simon, behold, Satan hath desired to have you, that he may sift you as wheat: but I have prayed for thee, that thy faith fail not: and when thou art converted, strengthen thy brethren.
—LUKE 22:31–32

The church of today doesn't remotely resemble the army of God going forth into battle. Cultural Christianity is a timid, backward religion that in no way resembles the militant, revolutionary church that God has called out of the world and into His kingdom of light.

The Greek word for church, *ecclesia*, refers to a "called-out people." Such a called-out church in the last day before eternity will find her identity in heaven, not on earth.

Such a called-out church will confront both the sins of commission and omission. Such a called-out church will refuse to allow adultery, immorality, pornography, violence, abuse, and murderous hate to exist within her ranks. Either those in her midst will radically surrender to Jesus Christ or they will be expunged from the ranks.

Such a called-out church is an army, not a club; an offensive weapon, not a cowering defender; a victor, not a victim. The devil is not on our backs; he's under our feet, which are bruising his head continually.

Such a called-out church insists on staying far away from the world that she has abandoned and is pushing in as close as possible to the Commander in Chief, Jesus Christ.

Such a called-out church foments a revolution in culture and will not retreat or quit until each opposing foe is either converted or put to flight. The *ecclesia* refuses to look back, go back, or even talk about the past land of slavery. Instead of being like the ancient Israelites in the wilderness who constantly murmured and complained, the End-Time, last-day-before-eternity church endures to the end.

The key word here is *endurance*. To endure means no compromise with the world...no quitting...no turning back...no immorality or impurity...no social sinning...and no sitting down to rest. Too many leaders today are crying out, "Church, take your rest," instead of barking the command, "Church, take up your weapons! Put on the armor of God! March! Fight! Endure to the end!"

The End-Time military force God is building in these final hours has no precedent in history, and Satan trembles at the forces that have been mustered by the King of kings and the Lord of lords. Demons shudder in the face of a host of Spirit-filled, born-again believers who know their authority and who know that Satan's time is short. So Satan is doing everything within his power to stifle or hinder us.

As I pointed out in the last chapter, the enemy attacks our endurance. The devil attacks us at every point of perceived weakness, hoping to discourage us. His aim is to convince us that we cannot persevere and thus we must quit. Satan attacks our endurance, hoping that we will compromise, bend, yield, and stumble. Now, I will explain Satan's rage at righteousness. I will expose his tactics and teach you how to overcome the devil when he sifts our lives. Peter will serve as our main example.

Satan understood Peter's potential. He watched him cast out demons and heal the sick. The devil saw Peter chisel away at his pride and begin to grow spiritually. When God's people grow, Satan cowers. As he tested Job, Satan also tried Peter and asked God for permission to sift the apostle in order to curb Peter's spiritual growth. Jesus explained, "Simon, Simon, behold, Satan hath desired to have you, that he may sift you as wheat: but I have prayed for thee, that thy faith fail not: and when thou art converted, strengthen thy brethren" (Luke 22:31–32).

What Satan didn't know was that his sifting would serve as a refining process and that God would use it to mature the disciple. Satan still believes that his sifting will destroy God's people even though time and again a saint's faith is refined when sifted. When you resist the devil and his sifting temptations, your faith will be stronger than before his attack.

When the heart of a devoted follower is immovable and committed in Christ, God will use the temptations of Satan to defeat him at his own game. And He will use them to make you wiser and bolder for Christ the next time around.

"Simon, Simon, behold, Satan hath desired to have you, that he may sift you as wheat...."

The actual translation of this passage shows that Satan requisitioned, or asked permission to sink his claws into, Peter. Temporarily, Peter succumbed to the sifting. As I mentioned in the last chapter, this mighty man of God fell prey to Satan's icy fear. As a result, Peter denied that he even knew Jesus—just as the Master had foretold.

Peter was down, but not out; confused, but undeterred. When the news of his Master's resurrection hit his ears, he was the first to race to the empty tomb. It was probably Peter who saw to the business arrangements of staying in the upper room where prayer invited the Holy Ghost's baptism. And it was Peter who was the first to embrace the Gentiles at the Roman Cornelius's home.

Why? Because Peter's faith had been built in the battle. And if God could build Peter in battle into the dynamo for Christ he became, He can certainly do it for you. We've looked at Paul's victorious example so far in this writing. Now, it's time to look at Peter.

PETER, SHUT UP!

Have you ever noticed that Peter got most of the press in the Gospel discourses? Over and over again throughout the disciples' adventures, it is Peter who seems to speak first. This natural leader was always the first to ask the important question or to make a stupid remark.

Remember? When Jesus announced His crucifixion and resurrection, it was Peter who rebuked Him: "Be it far from thee, Lord: this shall not be unto thee" (Matt. 16:22). Peter was also the first one to ask for the Lord's instruction when a teaching wasn't clear: "Lord, how oft shall my brother sin against me, and I forgive him? till seven times?" (Matt. 18:21).

We can identify with Peter. He was hungry to know God, but just a little overzealous and fearful when encountering the unknown. Until Christ's crucifixion, the Holy Spirit's treasure was only "with" him, not "in" him. So when Satan came to sift him, he was hoping, as he did with Judas, to take him out of the race.

Just as Paul was buffeted in his ministry with the things that he counted for his sake (shipwreck, snakebite, beatings, and imprisonment), so was Peter with violent mistreatment. *Buffet* means "to be violently mistreated." In Acts 4, Peter was jailed and accused of treason. In Acts 12, he was jailed again and scheduled for execution, but God sent His angel to release him. Along the way we see him preaching the first Christian sermon that brought three thousand men to the Lord in Acts 2. We see God using him to heal the lame man and bring another five thousand men to the Lord in Acts 4. Peter ministered the baptism in the Holy Ghost to thousands in Samaria, preached the first sermon to Gentiles in Acts 10, and defended Paul's ministry to the Gentiles before the Jerusalem council in Acts 15.

Do you think Satan would have allowed these exploits if he could have sifted Peter out of the picture in Luke 22? No. If he could have kept the well-meaning former fisherman struggling in the guilt of his initial failure of rejecting Jesus, he could have kept him out of the house in which Jesus appeared and dispensed His Holy Ghost (John 20:19). And he would have ensured Peter wouldn't have been anywhere near Christ's ascension to receive the invitation to the Spirit's power (Luke 24:49).

But Peter received straight A's in his many tests because of his committed heart. He had tasted and seen of the Lord's good mercy. So Satan's sifting following Jesus' capture in the garden only lasted a few days at best. Peter was down, but not out; confused, but not destroyed—because he knew the truth. Satan's intended destruction was used to refine his life.

Listen to the words of this refined vessel after he had been tested in the fire of obedience:

> Beloved, think it not strange concerning the fiery trial which is to try you, as though some strange thing happened unto you: But rejoice, inasmuch as ye are partakers of Christ's sufferings; that, when his glory shall be revealed, ye may be glad also with exceeding joy. If ye be reproached for the name of Christ, happy are ye; for the spirit of glory and of God resteth upon you: on their part he is evil spoken of, but on your part he is glorified.
>
> —1 PETER 4:12–14

You must understand the sifter's tactics. What is he after? Your endurance.

With what will he attack? "Now Peter sat without in the palace: and a damsel came unto him, saying, Thou also wast with Jesus of Galilee. But he denied before them all, saying, I know not what thou sayest" (Matt. 26:69–70).

In those fearsome hours surrounding Jesus Christ's crucifixion, Satan's murderous spirit of fear sent the disciples scattering in disarray. Every one of His chosen men except John was in hiding when Jesus breathed His last on the cross.

Peter himself was in the courtyard, wanting to be near Jesus. But Satan's fear had so filled his mind that Peter was filled with uncertainty and doubt. Satan's primary tool of sifting is *fear*, because fear produces doubt.

When you're going about God's business and a sudden thought starts to harass your thinking and push you into fear, you can know that is Satan wanting to draw you off your course. He attacks your endurance through the tool of deception. He sifts our minds with his words of deceit.

DECEIT: THE SIFTER'S WEAPON

Deceit is Satan's only weapon. "You missed it," he tried to con Peter. "You left a profitable fishing business to follow this mortal who had convinced you that He was the Messiah. And now He is being tried as a common criminal, and before long He'll be dead! You're next—as soon as they find you."

Satan can only attack through the tool of deception. Those who believe his lies quit with excuses that they use to try to justify their actions. They vainly believe that quitting is God's will.

First, the devil will sow a lie.

Next, he will sow another lie.

Then finally, he'll sow another lie.

And if on any one of them he can get you into discussion, he'll sow an even bigger lie until it escalates into a full-blown crisis that wasn't even there until he convinced you of it.

NAMING THE SIFTER

John names mankind's sifter as "the great dragon . . . that old serpent, called the Devil, and Satan, which deceiveth the whole world" (Rev. 12:9).

In 1 Peter 5:8 Peter calls him the "adversary" (Satan's translated name in the Hebrew); he admonished the church to be watchful, because the devil walks around as a roaring lion seeking whom he may devour.

Notice that Peter didn't say the devil walks around *devouring* whomever he may desire. No, the apostle says our adversary *seeks* whom he may devour: "Be sober, be vigilant; because your adversary the devil, as a roaring lion, walketh about, seeking whom he may devour."

So, Peter told us to be sober and to "watch out" with a calm and collected spirit, knowing the devil is a prowler and is seeking to sift.

I'm tired of hearing about saints who quit because they haven't been sober and watching. I'm tired of a sifted church that seeks safety in the suburbs and refuses to challenge the darkness that clothes cultural compromise and comfort. I'm tired of sifted choir members who want to sing in the choir until they find something else to do during Tuesday night rehearsal. I'm tired of sifted Sunday school teachers who teach for three weeks until they come out of the classroom with their hair frazzled and say, "This is too difficult for me."

I love them all, but I'm tired of seeing the devil get the victory in the lives of God's people.

APATHY: THE CROWN JEWEL OF THE TWENTIETH-CENTURY CHURCH

Apathy is the crown jewel of the twentieth-century church, and Satan is the one who polishes its deceptive fruit. He is the sifter who stalks his prey, then kills, steals, and destroys whomever he may. Satan knows that all he has to do is stop our forward motion, get us into a "reasonable discussion" of why this or that shouldn't be happening and how unfair life is, mix in just a little pity, and then we lose our endurance.

How it must dishearten God, if it were even possible for Him to be disheartened, when He sees His people shout and act as if they are full of the Holy Ghost, and then He watches as they are terrorized by some little demon that won't let them sleep.

The church is supposed to be a revolutionary movement—trained and tough. Second Chronicles 7:14 says:

> If my people, which are called by my name, shall humble themselves, and pray, and seek my face, and turn from their wicked ways; then will I hear from heaven, and will forgive their sin, and will heal their land.

This statement should put us on a collision course with our adversary. It lets us know that individually and corporately we are to be a conspicuous agent of change. Repentance, forgiveness, and change are what the gospel is all about. But Satan knows he has victory thwarted when we're hiding or sitting back, nursing the minor cuts and bruises he has inflicted. The truth is that we should be harassing him.

Satan uses lies to sift us. First of all, we should know that the adversary's sifting tools constitute nothing more than a lie. But I don't want to minimize this. The devil's lies can be as powerful as the truth when believed. They can push people to pull the trigger of a loaded .45 that they've personally pointed at their heads. They can send a world to war and fill prison cells every day. Lies can kill in more ways then one, if they aren't dealt with in the truth.

When you're down for the count and he says, "Quit!" remind him of the truth: "My God says I can do all things through Christ! So devil, I resist you in the name of Jesus. Turn and flee!"

When the devil tells you that you're a failure and tells you to give up, tell him: "I am the righteousness of God in Christ, and I'm forgiven; now hit the road!"

Remember, when Jesus told Peter that Satan had requested to sift him like wheat, Jesus also acknowledged He had prayed for Peter's faith. And He encouraged Peter to help his brethren once he had overcome the devil's lies. "And the Lord said, Simon, Simon, behold, Satan hath desired to have you, that he may sift you as wheat: but I have prayed for thee, that thy faith fail not: and when thou art converted, strengthen thy brethren" (Luke 22:31–32).

We must grab hold of the divine reality of Jesus Christ's high priestly prayer for those of us who have called upon His name. When we're in the heat of battle and the enemy's lies turn others against us unjustly, when we're working for God and Satan's sifting lies come to delude and stop us, we have a high priest who can sympathize with our human weakness, because He has been tempted in all points as we, yet without sin (Heb. 4:15).

Jesus understands what we're going through because He's been through it. But it is up to us to "come boldly unto the throne of grace, that we may obtain mercy, and find grace to help in time of need" (Heb. 4:16).

Accusation is a tactic used by the sifter. The sifter's lies often prove more effective when he can tell them through others and defame or degrade one of God's servants. Those who are working for God on more visible public scales are often those on Satan's accusing hit lists. He accused Jesus of insurrection, Paul of fleecing God's sheep, James and Peter of leading a rebellion, and every one of the other disciples as enemies of the state. "For the accuser of our brethren is cast down, which accused them before our God day and night" (Rev. 12:10).

The main lie he uses to keep thousands outside of the church is his accusation that we're all money-grubbing hypocrites. Just watch the media on any given day when they choose to air a story on this ministry or that church, and you will see his accusing agenda. You rarely hear about the good work we're doing for the needy in this world. You hear about the phonies and ripoffs. But rarely do you hear about the spiritual social work we are effectively ministering to the needy and lost every day.

Theodore Roosevelt said in a speech on April 23, 1910:

> It is not the critic who counts; not the man who points out how the strong man stumbles, or where the doer of deeds could have done them better. The credit belongs to the man who is actually in the arena, whose face is marred by dust and sweat and blood; who strives valiantly; who errs, and comes short again and again, because there is no effort without error and shortcoming; but who does actually strive to do the deed; who knows the great enthusiasms, the great devotions; who spends himself in a worthy cause; who at the best knows in the end the triumph of high achievement, and who at the worst, if he fails, at least fails while daring greatly, so that his place shall never be with those cold and timid souls who know neither victory nor defeat.

There are always more than enough critics of Christianity. Truth is deception's antidote, so if you're ever accused, simply stand in the truth.

We've got so many starters and so few finishers today in our milksop, feel-good church sanctuaries that dot America's landscape. No, they don't reject God's sovereignty and His saving grace, but when the enemy comes at them with accusations and personal confusion, they buy into his deception and quit.

I see laymen and ministers who come to our annual camp meeting to get recharged. They return to their prayer closets for a while, but before long the devil returns and the pressure around them pushes them to the brink of failure again. Some of them I never see again because of progressive isolation.

Isolation is another of the sifter's tactics. The devil seeks to isolate us. He will do what he can do to isolate God's people, just as he isolated Elijah after Elijah defeated the prophets of Baal. Remember, the Spirit of God had so mightily fallen upon this prophet that he personally killed four hundred fifty prophets of Baal. At Elijah's word, no rain fell on Israel for three years; at the final showdown, Elijah destroyed Baal worship in Israel after God sent fire from heaven to prove His reality (1 Kings 18).

Then, after all of this—Satan "informed" him through a messenger that Jezebel was going to kill him—and he ran off into the wilderness on a pity party, fearing for his life.

In 1 Kings 19 we see the prophet complaining that he was the only one willing to stand up to the devil. If the sifter could get such a mighty man of God separated with one barbed-edged lie, and if such a man as this Tishbite who called fire down from heaven on more than one occasion could be sifted through Satan's deception, then we would do well to learn from his tactics.

Jesus said Satan was the father of all lies, that he was a murderer from the beginning, and that no truth could be found in him (John 8:44). If he can sift God's people into isolation, he can delude them into oblivion.

So when Elijah cried on Mount Horeb that he was the only one left in Israel that served and loved God, the Lord immediately set him straight. God informed Elijah of seven thousand others who were also working for Him, and then He sent him on another mission to ensure that Elijah's forward motion wouldn't be stopped as the enemy planned. "Go anoint Jehu king of Israel and find your successor, Elisha. Now go, Elijah, and don't look back. I am with you." (See 1 Kings 19:15–21.)

LAZY, DECEIVED SAINTS

The sifter will also do what he can to accommodate your flesh to make you lazy. I was talking with a businessman recently who told me only 2 percent of today's work force in America require no supervision. Eighty-four percent of our work force require constant supervision. Why? Because they're lazy. "Why bother with your output?" Satan tells them. "Let the owners worry about it; it's not your concern."

And the lazy are in the church. You can see so many of God's people expend their energy going to meeting after meeting until their forehead is smeared with five layers of oil, looking like a greased pig. But they're too lazy to get up and walk the floor at night, praying and confessing the Word. The spiritually lazy remain biblical illiterates because they will not study the Bible for themselves.

The Bible says when the enemy comes in like a flood (to check your endurance), the Spirit of the Lord will raise up a standard against Him (Isa. 59:19). And that standard is God's Word. But we must recognize and apply our energy to studying, seeking, and speaking His Word when the enemy comes around.

Satan attacks the Bible because it is the only document on earth that exposes who he is. It is only in God's Word that men can learn how to overcome the devil and his tactics.

Paul tells us to put on the whole armor of God, including the sword of the Spirit (which is the Word of God), the belt of truth, the breastplate of righteousness, the shield of faith, and the helmet of salvation—all weapons of truth to defeat the sifter's lies (Eph. 6:13–17). Paul continues, telling us to "[pray] always with all prayer and supplication in the Spirit, and watching thereunto with all perseverance and supplication for all saints" (v. 18).

Peter instructs us, "As newborn babes, desire the sincere milk of the word, that ye may grow thereby: If so be ye have tasted that the Lord is gracious" (1 Pet. 2:2–3).

Paul tells us:

For when for the time ye ought to be teachers, ye have need

that one teach you again which be the first principles of the oracles of God; and are become such as have need of milk, and not of strong meat. For every one that useth milk is unskilful in the word of righteousness: for he is a babe. But strong meat belongeth to them that are of full age, even those who by reason of use have their senses exercised to discern both good and evil.

—Hebrews 5:12–14

Elijah found the Word of God in the still quiet voice on Horeb, and that is where we will find Him, too.

Tried, Tested, and True

I went to the hospital bed of my beloved pastor, Lester Sumrall, during the last hours of his life. He had obeyed God in building television stations. As those television stations worth ten million dollars burned to the ground, I watched him stand firm against the attacks of the devil, standing up in the pulpit two hours later to preach. I watched him bury his wife and start a ten-city tour the next day in which he preached twice a day for a week and a half. I watched him stand when men reviled, persecuted, laughed, and mocked this tested man of faith. Through it all I watched Lester Sumrall keep his eyes on Jesus as he refused to give Satan one day of his life.

How glorious it was when his denomination said, "Sumrall, you're fifty, and you're finished," and he pushed on to raise up a church of six thousand people, a food organization that blesses the world, twelve television stations, and a Bible college.

Here was a man who understood the deceptive ploys of Satan and went forward after every attack. He endured and set an example for us all. Lester Sumrall always came away from the devil's sifting stronger to meet new tasks.

Let's return to Peter. This rough, tough fisherman straight off the Galilee docks was always the first one to pop off at the mouth and show his ignorance. But as he spent time with the Refiner and endured all of Satan's attacks, Peter grew into one of the finest

Christian examples revealed in the Scriptures.

Observe how Peter protested when Jesus prophesied that the disciples would desert him. Peter claimed that he would never forsake Jesus. Watch him rebuke Jesus when informed of His impending crucifixion and, as a result, earn Christ's rebuke as Satan himself. Then read Peter's first and second epistles and experience how God's refining process matured and shaped this man:

> Blessed be the God and Father of our Lord Jesus Christ, which according to his abundant mercy hath begotten us again unto a lively hope by the resurrection of Jesus Christ from the dead, to an inheritance incorruptible, and undefiled, and that fadeth not away, reserved in heaven for you, who are kept by the power of God through faith unto salvation ready to be revealed in the last time. Wherein ye greatly rejoice, though now for a season, if need be, ye are in heaviness through manifold temptations: that the trial of your faith, being much more precious than of gold that perisheth, though it be tried with fire, might be found unto praise and honour and glory at the appearing of Jesus Christ: whom having not seen, ye love; in whom, though now ye see him not, yet believing, ye rejoice with joy unspeakable and full of glory: receiving the end of your faith, even the salvation of your souls.
>
> —1 PETER 1:3–9

Though he had many wonderful opportunities to drop out of the race, Peter was no quitter. He could have returned to his fishing business and attended church, like anyone of us when the going got tough. But this man would have rather died. The treasure of God's Holy Spirit deposited in his earthen vessel was empowering Peter to do God's will, overcome the enemy, and go forward in God's purpose for the church. Tradition tells us that Peter was crucified upside down, at his request, because he felt unworthy to be martyred upright as his Lord. When Peter finished his course, in the end he heard Jesus' glorious words, "Well done, thou good and faithful servant!"

That's what life is about! Pleasing God through fulfilling His will and receiving His promises while running our course!

Have you been experiencing the sifting of Satan? Have you been sensing a lie buzzing around your head, which has no substance of proof? Has someone accused you of wrongdoing, when in reality you've only been doing good? Maybe you've allowed yourself to be isolated, and it's been months, even years, since you've been in church. If this is you, seek a quiet place right after you finish this chapter. Rehearse the truths you've learned in it, and then find a truth in the Bible for every one of your adversary's lies.

LIES, LIES, LIES

Lies are the tools of the sifter. But God's truth and light exposes every lie. For the sifter's sickness, God promises healing. For the sifter's depression, God promises joy. For the sifter's arrogance, God promises humility. For the sifter's lethargy, God promises strength. But it is up to us to believe God's good report.

There are a shocking number of Christians in America today who don't believe the Bible is absolute truth. The sifter has convinced them they can edit, cut out, and paraphrase the Old and New Testaments together with Molech and Baal in a sort of religious stew that appeases everyone—that is, everyone except the Lord God.

But the last-days military force God is building in earth's closing days is separating itself from these devious doctrines. No longer are we bowing to the heretical notions that God is the author of failure and humanism. He is building in battle the remnant who know the lateness of the hour and that Satan can only roar as he watches our triumphs of faith.

This is why James tells us to "count it all joy when [we] fall into divers temptations; knowing that the trying of [our] faith worketh patience. But let patience have her perfect work, that [we] may be perfect and entire, wanting nothing" (James 1:2–4).

And it is also why Peter tells us to "gird up the loins of [our] mind[s], be sober, and hope to the end for the grace that is to be brought unto [us] at the revelation of Jesus Christ" (1 Pet. 1:13).

Whenever the devil attacks, remember these truths.

- Satan uses lies to sift you. Ground yourself in God's truth.

- Satan will accuse and condemn you. Remember that there is no condemnation for those in Christ Jesus.

- Satan will try to isolate you. Stay in constant fellowship with the saints.

- Satan will tempt you to become lazy and apathetic. Remain zealous for the Lord.

- Satan will try to break your endurance and persuade you to quit. Stand firm on the rock of Christ to the end.

The last day before eternity approaches quickly. Expect the ploys of the sifter, and stay steady to crush his head! "And the God of peace shall bruise Satan under your feet shortly. The grace of our Lord Jesus Christ be with you. Amen" (Rom. 16:20).

Prepare yourself for the fires of Christian conquest that will build leadership like no other forming process once we choose to endure to the finish line the course God has set before us.

_____

_____

_____

_____

_____

_____

_____

_____

_____

_____

_____

_____

_____

_____

_____

_____

_____

_____

_____

_____

 FIVE

THE FIRE'S
PURIFYING POWER

Beloved, think it not strange concerning the fiery trial which is to try you, as though some strange thing happened unto you: But rejoice, inasmuch as ye are partakers of Christ's sufferings; that, when his glory shall be revealed, ye may be glad also with exceeding joy.

—1 PETER 4:12–13

The final hours of the last day before eternity tick by, drawing us into the fiery trials of faith. Will you be singed or refined, consumed or consecrated, left as ashes or fine gold? In ancient history—long before Saddam Hussein built gaudy castles in the land between two rivers, the Tigris and the Euphrates—a world-ruling monarch, Nebuchadnezzar, had built a mighty capital city called Babylon with wondrous hanging gardens and a loathsome idol. The king's command to worship a stone image would push three God-fearers to a precipice overlooking their last day before eternity.

The gargantuan idol towered alongside Babylon's western wall, glistening in the afternoon's sunlight as its stern expression ominously surveyed its fashioner's domain.

"You will not bow?" asked the king one last time.

"We will not; our God will deliver us," said Shadrach, Meshach, and Abednego, who were bound from head to foot with rope.

"Open the furnace!" the king angrily commanded. "Throw these three troublemakers to their deaths for rebelling against my command. Let the world see what awaits any who refuse to bow to my honor!"

You know the story. "Bow or burn!" was the satanic ultimatum given these three remnant followers of God. But the three Hebrew youth did neither as they stood firm in the face of a circumstance that threatened their lives. They knew the God of all creation, and they knew He wouldn't forsake them in the face of their own deaths.

Flames exploded out of the glowing furnace, consuming the soldiers who obeyed the king's command.

"You have killed your best commanders, King! You have . . . "

"One more word and I will kill you too, Captain!" rebuked the king as he cut the detail commander off.

Then suddenly, the flames subsided, allowing a view inside the furnace. Nebuchadnezzar rubbed his eyes in disbelief as he peered through the smoke of his soldier's smoldering corpses. Shadrach, Meshach, and Abednego could be seen—with a fourth brilliant figure—walking around untouched by the flames inside!

Nebuchadnezzar stood dumbstruck by this eye-popping experience, which would serve as the first of many that would eventually change his life:

> Then Nebuchadnezzar spake, and said, Blessed be the God of Shadrach, Meshach, and Abednego, who hath sent his angel, and delivered his servants that trusted in him, and have changed the king's word, and yielded their bodies, that they might not serve nor worship any god, except their own God. Therefore I make a decree, That every people, nation, and language, which speak any thing amiss against the God of Shadrach, Meshach, and Abednego, shall be cut in pieces, and their houses shall be made a dunghill: because there is no other God that can deliver after this sort. Then the king promoted Shadrach, Meshach, and Abednego, in the province of Babylon.
> —DANIEL 3:28–30

As previously mentioned in the last chapter, when the heart of a devoted follower is immovable and committed in Christ, God will use the temptations of Satan to defeat him at his own game. And He will use those same temptations to make us wiser and more discerning the next time around.

The very idol Nebuchadnezzar fashioned to take life in Babylon would be used as the first leg in his own conversion. Within a year, he would be living as a wild beast in the forest, fulfilling one last divine dream. Then in seven years, he would come to his senses, a convert of the Hebrew God of Shadrach, Meshach, and Abednego:

> Now I Nebuchadnezzar praise and extol and honour the King of heaven, all whose works are truth, and his ways judgment: and those that walk in pride he is able to abase.
>
> —DANIEL 4:37

WHAT THE ENEMY INTENDS FOR EVIL, GOD WILL USE FOR GOOD

When Daniel was later accused by Darius's counselors of offending the king's decree, he was thrown to the lions. But the "fourth man" shut the lions' mouths, and those counselors were eaten alive (Daniel 6).

After Joseph was brutally sold into slavery by his jealous brothers, he was faithful in Potiphar's home as his household steward. Then one day, Potiphar's wife attempted to seduce him. When Joseph refused to give in, she accused him of rape and had him imprisoned. But that "fourth man" went behind bars with Joseph, and one day he was released and promoted to Pharaoh's right-hand man.

Joseph's attitude, which was Paul's attitude (love "beareth all things, believeth all things, hopeth all things, endureth all things" [1 Cor. 13:7]), enabled him to endure his mistreatment and, in the end, turn it for good. On the day that he finally faced his treacherous brothers, he was fully aware of his trial's overall redemptive plan. "And Joseph said unto them, Fear not: for am I in the place of God? But as for you, ye thought evil against me; but God meant it unto good, to bring to pass, as it is this day, to save much people alive" (Gen. 50:19–20).

What a testimony we have of the toughness and sold-out commitment of these called-out, front-line warriors of God in the Scriptures. These were men of steel and velvet who stood tough as nails in the face of adversity and won souls for their courage along the way.

Of course, this didn't stop Satan's plans of destroying their lives. He didn't want Shadrach, Meshach, Abednego, and Daniel unsettling his kingdom in Babylon. He didn't want Joseph ever to leave the pit or prison. And he doesn't want you unsettling his work down the street or even in your home.

If Satan has to kill to stop the forward motion of God's people, he is still free in many lands to do it today. Because America has turned her head away from God to serve the corroding god of mammon, we turn our heads away from the killing fields of Red China and Sudan where Christians are brutally murdered and sold into slavery because of their Christian faith. We forget that millions of Christians were murdered with the Jews and other dissidents in Hitler's concentration camps and in the gulags of communist Russia.

We don't preach much on the fact that every one of the twelve disciples lost their lives for professing their faith. Tradition says John was boiled in oil, but that he was supernaturally spared. The remaining disciples (barring Judas) were all imprisoned and killed—for birthing the New Testament church! The truth is that we are refined by fire before entering eternity.

Now, don't think that I am advocating or glorifying martyrdom, because I'm not. What I am saying is this: In these last days of the church as we head into the last day before eternity, more and more opportunities will present themselves to be thrown into Nebuchadnezzar's fire, Daniel's den, and Pharaoh's prison. We may not be confronted with a literal bow-or-burn situation, but we may face demands for our compromise at the expense of certain freedoms that America once guaranteed.

Our Christian Bill of Rights in America began a revision of powerful godless forces in 1962 when atheist Madalyn Murray O'Hair worked to remove God from the classrooms of our public schools. Since then, many modern educators have banded together to write God out of American history in a spiritual and academic "dumbing down" process in our public schools. Hinduism, Buddhism, witchcraft, and many other abominable false religions are preached as noble facts and theories. Yet, God and His Ten Commandments are forbidden, because of their power to change.

Let there be no mistake about the fact that those with the same spirit as Nebuchadnezzar have been stoking the fires of his furnace in America since 1962. The American Civil Liberties Union would like nothing better than to eradicate Christianity from the American landscape just as their communist forerunners did in Russia and China earlier in this century. Many court battles waged against Christian persecution have so far found sympathy in the U.S. Constitution. But those days could eventually come to an end. And if they do, so what?

It never ceases to amaze me that Paul wrote Romans 13, his stirring Christian citizenship doctrine, while imprisoned by the very government the Holy Spirit commanded him to respect. I still get angry at the antics of Washington, D.C., but Paul could write these words while awaiting his execution!

> Let every soul be subject unto the higher powers. For there is no power but of God: the powers that be are ordained of God. Whosoever therefore resisteth the power, resisteth the ordinance of God: and they that resist shall receive to themselves damnation. For rulers are not a terror to good works, but to the evil. Wilt thou then not be afraid of the power? Do that which is good, and thou shalt have praise of the same: For he is the minister of God to thee for good.
>
> —ROMANS 13:1–4

Paul's mission was to appear before the recognized leader of the world in his day, Caesar, to preach the gospel of Christ, and he was beheaded for his obedience. But the church was birthed everywhere he went along his Rome-bound way. And this should be our attitude, too.

No matter what awaits the church in these last days before eternity—come new zoning regulations that forbid home church groups, hellish new tax codes, or hell and high water in any other fashion or way, the fires of persecution will refine our faith in battle as victors. And many will be saved from the fires of hell.

THE FIERY ATTACK OF THE ENEMY

If Satan can stop the church's forward motion, he can block us from fulfilling God's plan. So first of all, let's remember again the sifter's tactics.

What is he after? Your endurance. What will he attack it with? Difficulties, but most of all, fear and doubt.

Some fear will arise from actual physical attacks and persecution while other fear will arise from deception intended to distract us from God's mission and plan. Today in America, we face more the deceptive fear that enslaves our minds and renders our lives powerless to live boldly as light and salt in the world.

All Shadrach, Meshach, and Abednego had to do to avoid Nebuchadnezzar's raging furnace was bow to his image. All Daniel had to do to avoid the lions' den was stop praying. All Joseph had to do to avoid prison and possible execution was submit to the adulterous seduction of Potiphar's wife. All Paul had to do in Ephesus was stop his preaching so the idol makers could continue to profit from their craft. All Peter and James had to do in Jerusalem to avoid imprisonment and execution was to "speak no more to anyone in Jesus' name."

All you have to do to avoid the possible repercussion of your local school board, neighbors, and family members is keep your mouth shut.

When your little boy's Bible is confiscated at school on the grounds of "separation of church and state"—all you have to do to avoid his ongoing persecution and possible suspension is *keep your mouth shut.*

When your senator sponsors homosexual legislation that would grant perversion "civil rights"—all you have to do to avoid politically correct harassment and persecution is *keep your mouth shut.*

When you're feeling the prompting of the Holy Spirit in the supermarket checkout line to tell the man in front of you, "Jesus died for your sins, and He is the answer to your problem"—all you have to do to avoid a scene is *keep your mouth shut.*

When you're prompted of the Holy Spirit to visit the down-trodden, broken, and deserted single mother or drug addict to tell them Jesus is the answer to their every need and their child's sickness—all you have to do avoid their possible rejection is bow to Satan's fear and *keep your mouth shut.*

When you're teaching Sunday school and the Holy Spirit prompts you to break through that religious spirit of the unbelieving parents who drop off their children to make up for their spiritual neglect—all you have to do to keep their children in Sunday school and avoid offending them is *keep your mouth shut.*

When you're believing for that family member to finally come to the Lord in a strong and consistent way—all you have to do to avoid their possible rejection is refuse the Holy Spirit's prompting and *keep your mouth shut.*

If you keep your mouth shut, you will be where Satan wants you—in the land of waffling compromise in fear of his tactics and lies. But for every unspoken word of truth any of us withhold because of Satan's deceptions and fear, a soul is forfeited to the regions of hell. Not only that, but when we bow to Satan's idols of fear and deceit, our faith becomes weakened and we become hypocrites and a make-believe world of church and play.

DON'T FORGET THE FOURTH MAN!

> But in a great house there are not only vessels of gold and of
> silver, but also of wood and of earth; and some to honour, and
> some to dishonour.
>
> —2 TIMOTHY 2:20

Fire is the final hardening process in the potter's house of vessel perfection. So when our obedience to the Spirit's prompting may happen to cause the flames of hell to ignite around us, they will only serve to refine our hearts. But we never walk through them alone. When we are scorched by the fires of life's opposing circumstances, that fourth Man, who kept the flames from consuming Shadrach, Meshach, and Abednego, will be there to share our flames. Jesus will be there to work with our hearts and form us as vessels for noble use.

Peter knew fire's power to purify and perfect: "That the trial of your faith, being much more precious than of gold that perisheth, though it be tried with fire, might be found unto praise and honour and glory at the appearing of Jesus Christ" (1 Pet. 1:7).

And it didn't take the apostle long in his gospel-unfriendly country to expect it at any time in any place:

> Beloved, think it not strange concerning the fiery trial which is to try you, as though some strange thing happened unto you: but rejoice, inasmuch as ye are partakers of Christ's sufferings; that, when his glory shall be revealed, ye may be glad also with exceeding joy. If ye be reproached for the name of Christ, happy are ye; for the spirit of glory and of God resteth upon you: on their part he is evil spoken of, but on your part he is glorified.
>
> —1 PETER 4:12–14

Notice that Peter said to "think it not strange" when the fiery trials of life come our way. To think something is strange is to think it "out of the ordinary," or it is to misunderstand the purpose of the Christian life's siftings and trials.

Church tradition holds that Peter was crucified upside down at his request when his martyrdom was at hand because he felt himself unworthy to die upright as his Lord. But I am absolutely assured that Peter didn't stretch out his arms to be led where he didn't want to go, as Jesus prophesied in John 21:18, until his course was finished.

Once, while awaiting his execution in the scorching fires of Herod's prison, an angel awoke Peter, released his chains, and led him to safety (Acts 12).

When Paul and Silas felt the scorching heat of a Roman jail in Philippi, the prison shook to its core and every prison door opened, bringing the prison jailer to his knees in repentant prayer (Acts 16).

When in scorching heat Paul's antagonists in Lystra stoned him for healing a lame man, God raised him from the dead to continue his mission (Acts 14).

Every time Jesus was cornered by His scorching antagonists, He walked right through the midst of them, and He kept on walking until His mission was *done* (Luke 4; John 7).

THE CRUCIBLE'S COMFORT IS *REST*

What was the common denominator that each of these men shared in overcoming their fiery trials? *Rest!* If Peter had rejected his calling and the Pharisees recognized him on the docks and had him imprisoned, the backslidden fisherman would have probably gone to jail in misery. Peter wrote, "For it is better, if the will of God be so, that ye suffer for well doing, than for evil doing" (1 Pet. 3:17).

Everywhere that Peter went and everything he did after his commissioning to feed God's flock was in the perfect will of God (John 21:15–16). It is only in His will, yoked to Christ and in the process of fulfilling God's perfect placement, that God's holy people experience His rest.

> Come unto me, all ye that labour and are heavy laden, and I will give you rest. Take my yoke upon you, and learn of me; for I am meek and lowly in heart: and ye shall find rest unto your souls. For my yoke is easy, and my burden is light.
> —MATTHEW 11:28–30

Peter learned early in his calling that suffering at the hands of the unrighteous was to share in the sufferings of Christ: "And they departed from the presence of the council, rejoicing that they were counted worthy to suffer shame for his name. And daily in the temple, and in every house, they ceased not to teach and preach Jesus Christ" (Acts 5:41–42).

It was Peter's full confidence in the fact of his mission's sovereign alignment with God's perfect will that he was able to sleep restfully the night before his scheduled execution. And I mean, he didn't just sleep—he slept while chained between two soldiers! God's rest tempered Peter's calling as he peacefully endured his fiery ordeal. He wasn't angry or confused about his situation. He wasn't unsure of God's will in the matter. So, he slept like a baby in Herod's jail the night before his scheduled beheading, knowing that even if he died, he would rejoice in eternal rest with the Lord.

But Peter didn't die. In fact, an angel delivered him right out from under the noses of the guards he was chained between! So he pressed on again in the perfect will of his Master, continuing his ministry to Christ's flock.

When the scorching fires of life's trials ignite, they will refine those enjoying His rest.

The Lord's yoking and promised rest is why Peter could encourage us to "think it not strange" when the fires of life's trials suddenly ignite.

Knowing their purpose and placement in Nebuchadnezzar's court was why Shadrach, Meshach, and Abednego could walk fearlessly into Nebuchadnezzar's fire. Because of their rest in God's placement and care, they could say, "If it be so, our God whom we serve is able to deliver us from the burning fiery furnace, and he will deliver us out of thine hand, O king. But if not, be it known unto thee, O king, that we will not serve thy gods, nor worship the golden image which thou hast set up" (Dan. 3:17–18).

The Lord's rest is why Paul could say all things were for his sake. He understood that his obedience to the perfect will of God (including beatings and imprisonments) was far better than living in the most palatial quarters available to him in his former life as a Pharisee. Paul understood that the sufferings he endured for Christ far outweighed any earthly stature or reputation he formerly enjoyed in the world. In fact, in the Book of Philippians he called them *dung*. "Yea doubtless, and I count all things but loss for the excellency of the knowledge of Christ Jesus my Lord: for whom I have suffered the loss of all things, and do count them but dung, that I may win Christ" (Phil. 3:8).

So the rest of God is the tempering factor in our crucible times of the Christian life.

As horrible as it may sound, church history teaches us that the Roman executioners of many early Christians were saved when they witnessed the martyr's rest and joy in dying. Peter was imprisoned because Herod saw that it pleased the Jews when he imprisoned and beheaded the apostle James. So James did go to prison to meet his death! And I am convinced that James slept restfully the night before he lost his head, just as Peter did, because James knew whose he was and what he was doing.

No Compromise!

Do you know whose you are . . . and what you are doing? If you do, you can expect a little scorching. But you can also expect God to walk through it with you. Compromise is the language of the devil. So when you refuse to compromise, you may feel some heat. But as you stay steady in God's will, He will humiliate the devil while exalting Christ's cause.

Remember, all you have to do is keep your mouth shut to appease the Nebuchadnezzars of our day. As the day before eternity enters its final hours and revival fires blaze across our land, maybe Nebuchadnezzar will build a new idol. Possibly your boss will tell you to bow or burn for not attending your company's New Age seminar. Maybe that tempter or temptress down the hall will finally corner you in the hall. Maybe, just maybe, an unredeemable Supreme Court and fallen U. S. Congress will even command the worship of all "illegal" church groups. And if so, *stand*.

Stand in the rest of God's calling in your life and you will endure the fire. You may be singed and scorched as God refines your faith in the flames, but you won't be consumed. There will be a fourth Man in the furnace with you, and He will see you through the fire and usher you into eternity.

Six

PRAYER: A HEART ATTITUDE

And shall not God avenge his own elect, which cry day and night
unto him, though he bear long with them? I tell you that he will
avenge them speedily. Nevertheless when the Son of man cometh,
shall he find faith on the earth?

—LUKE 18:7–8

Living in the last day before eternity requires constant and unceasing prayer. Is that possible in the midst of a world that robs our time and infects our brains with cyberspace images of decadence and iniquity?

When the fires of God's calling get hot and the enemy of our soul is there to fan the flames as he sifts those around us to attack and defame—that is the time to crawl up into our Father's lap to seek Him in fervent prayer. It is within life's trying flames that we are forged into champions adequate for the Master's use. It is faith that understands the reasons of our attack, and it is faith that seeks God's redeeming help when we're squared off in the battle's fray.

We are besieged daily by differing thoughts that try to scramble our brains and differing situations that require God's thoughts to help us see and move in His anointed ways. So we must come to know Him through His Word and consecrated prayer. Prayer is the key to conforming us into His image when the fires of life threaten to consume our thoughts. It is within those seasons of interaction with our Holy Father in the good and troubled times that His loving compassion forms and encourages us in Spirit and in truth.

It is our prayerful fellowship with God that will always see us through and give us direction. But, the proper path to prayer and godly fellowship is a controversial subject. Some believe that everything in life is predestined; they claim anything that happens on any given day is the holy, revealed will of God.

So why pray?

Others seek to pray their way out of God's will with special quotes and phrases from the Bible that refute the reality they are facing.

Understanding that God is sovereign, we push forward into God's perfect will with the word of our testimony that holds to the truths of Scripture, and we pray accordingly. Every thought that you think and every word that you say is a potential curse or powerful prayer. And the devil knows it! When we take the sword of the Spirit and command Satan to flee, he knows where the door is and rushes out it as quickly as possible.

LIVING IN THE MIND-SET OF PRAYER

Not only is prayer a spoken exclamation of God's Word, it is also an attitude, a mind-set that is the mind of Christ. Prayer is a mind-set that fosters patience, rejects defeat, and presses forward with no retreat. It is the attitude disclosed by Jesus in His parable of the unrighteous judge and widow. In this powerful parable, Jesus taught that men *ought to pray always*. And because He taught this, many have found it confusing.

"Certainly the Bible can't mean what it's saying here," many say. "How am I to pray always? How much of the time is always anyway? Is it all but ten minutes, two or three hours? Does it mean to pray twenty hours a day?"

So let's look at the parable, and then address the confusion.

And he spake a parable unto them to this end, that men ought always to pray, and not to faint; saying, There was in a city a judge, which feared not God, neither regarded man: and there was a widow in that city; and she came unto him, saying, Avenge me of mine adversary. And he would not for a while: but afterwards he said within himself, Though I fear not God, nor regard man; yet because this widow troubleth me, I will avenge her, lest by her continual coming she weary me. And the Lord said, Hear what the unjust judge saith. And shall not God avenge his own elect, which cry day and night unto him, though he bear long with them? I tell you that he will avenge them speedily. Nevertheless when the Son of man cometh, shall he find faith on the earth?

—LUKE 18:1–8

Jesus painted a character in this parable of an unrighteous judge who cared nothing for man or God. He pitted this self-centered, nasty figure against a frail, helpless widow who had been defrauded according to law. Just exactly how many times this widow petitioned the judge for legal justification isn't made clear. What is made clear is that she approached him so consistently that she "troubled" him to the point of finally granting her request. Then Jesus made a comparison: "And the Lord said, Hear what the unjust judge saith. And shall not God avenge his own elect, which cry day and night unto him, though he bear long with them? I tell you that he will avenge them speedily" (vv. 6–8).

In this parable, Jesus taught that consistency will bring even the unrighteous magistrates in a land to their knees, but how much more will our righteous God avenge His elect who cry to him day and night. Or, *pray always* as the parable intends.

Now I don't know many people who pray always. To understand this parable, we must refer to Paul's teaching in 1 Thessalonians, and then come back to Luke.

In 1 Thessalonians 5:17, Paul tells us to "pray without ceasing." Now, I have seasons and habits of prayer, just as you hopefully do. But I don't come down to the church and stay on my face in prayer twenty-four hours a day. This is what "ought to pray always" and "pray without ceasing" would seem to indicate on the surface. But there is a deeper meaning. There is a deeper dimension of prayer than mere time that Jesus was teaching in His Luke 18 parable, which Paul reminds us of in 1 Thessalonians: Prayer is not only a consecrated time of seeking; it is also an understanding of purpose, and this puts prayer on another dimension.

We have thought that prayer was kneeling down and folding our hands or closing ourselves in a closet. We've developed our rudiments, prayed through the Lord's Prayer, stood in the sanctuary with hands lifted up, and all the rest of these things, and we're called that prayer. But prayer is more than uttering words or these many calisthenics of spiritual prayer. All these things have their purpose. Yet the most important thing is knowing *your* purpose. It is knowing and fully living out your blood-bought life as a Spirit-filled believer, directing every waking day toward that purpose in life. It involves a mind-set that continually seeks those things that are above: "If ye then be risen with Christ, seek those things which are above, where Christ sitteth on the right hand of God. Set your affection on things above, not on things on the earth" (Col. 3:1–2).

Setting our "affection on things above" isn't some sort of heavenly escapism whereby we walk around with our heads in the clouds "hoping" to be removed from the battle by the Rapture. Paul is simply telling us to remain in a holy, consecrated mind-set that perceives any given situation on any given day from heaven's noble perspective. He defines that perspective in many different ways in his writings, but especially in Philippians 4:8:

> Finally, brethren, whatsoever things are true, whatsoever things are honest, whatsoever things are just, whatsoever things are pure, whatsoever things are lovely, whatsoever things are of good report; if there be any virtue, and if there be any praise, think on these things.

So, in essence, the kind of prayer Jesus and Paul are talking about involves living on a victorious dimension that does involve words and times of consecration. But when your mind is renewed and thinking in the heavenly realm, and your every word flows out of a heart of relationship, you will find that, just as in worship, you will be praying twenty-four hours a day.

HOLINESS AND PURPOSE:
THE TRUE ISSUES OF PRAYER

God is calling us to live out His purpose as a holy people in this last day before eternity. Let me give you an example of what that means. Worship doesn't necessarily involve the lifting of our hands in a church service while singing a slow song. This is a style of worship, but it is not necessarily the substance of worship. Worship involves more than raising our hands, clapping, dancing, or even prostrating ourselves face down before a holy God. Worship and praying without ceasing go together hand in hand.

As saints of the most high God, we are called to be holy and sanctified, especially in our prayer life. And when we are truly holy and separated unto our heavenly Father's work, when we are fulfilling that *purpose* for which He sanctified us in the first place, we will have our minds set on the things above.

The hummingbird buries its head in the tulip, and God says, "That's worship." The eagle flies to the far-flung winds of the morning, and God says, "That's worship." Why? Because they are fulfilling their purpose.

Conversely, it would not be worship if an eagle were to put its head into a tulip or if a hummingbird were to fly to snow-capped mountain peaks. So, purpose is the mission, and the mission involves prayer. And our prayers will be effectual when we are living on God's dimension of truth.

The purpose Jesus gave for always praying was so men would "faint not." When you've fainted, you're paralyzed. You can't move. You're beaten, broken down, and helpless—and that's where the devil wants you. But those who pray without ceasing through a rock solid knowledge of their purpose in life and a godly attitude about it don't faint or give up. So, praying and fainting are mutually exclusive.

The widow in Christ's parable was tenacious, coming before the unrighteous judge every day. She could have fainted by taking the unrighteous judge's unrighteous decision and resolving herself to her hopeless plight. She could have set her mind on the situation and said, "What's the difference? I know I have been illegally violated of my rights under the law, but this judge doesn't care...so what can I do?"

But she didn't. She knew she was right and had truth on her side, so she continually approached him, saying, "Avenge me of mine adversary! Avenge me of mine adversary! Avenge me of mine adversary! Avenge me of mine adversary! Avenge me of mine adversary!" And the unrighteous judge *would not for a while,* ". . . but afterwards he said within himself, Though I fear not God, nor regard man; yet because this widow troubleth me, I will avenge her, lest by her continual coming she weary me" (Luke 18:4–5).

What this reprobate judge finally agreed to is not the attitude of our righteous heavenly Father. Jesus simply used His graphic illustration to juxtapose the true nature of God when He said, "Hear what the unjust judge saith. And shall not God avenge his own elect, which cry day and night unto him, though he bear long with them? I tell you that he will avenge them speedily" (vv. 6–8).

"Your heavenly Father is not like this judge!" Jesus taught. "If the unrighteous forces of this earth can be moved by God's elect through their forward-moving lifestyle of heavenly minded faith, how much more will your Father avenge and justify you every day as you continually seek Him?"

And He called that faith. But then He ended the parable with a question: "Nevertheless when the Son of man cometh, shall he find faith on the earth?" (v. 8).

Jesus taught His disciples to fight because the Christian life is a fight. He taught us in this parable that life isn't going to sprout petunias and tulips. There are unrighteous forces out there that will attack our blood-bought rights as God's children and will try to defraud us illegally. This unrighteous judge didn't regard man or fear God, but he had to give in to the widow's commitment and tenacity.

There are no pew-warming, Sunday morning, go-to-church loopholes in authentic prayer. This calling we follow is a struggle. It's a battle. And it will only be won by those who lose their life in

Christ, as Jesus commanded in Luke 9: "And he said to them all, If any man will come after me, let him deny himself, and take up his cross daily, and follow me" (Luke 9:23).

It is only in following our Lord wholly, in sanctified holiness, that we gain His strength to overcome in the battle's fray.

This thing is not to the weak and frail! This thing is to the fierce and ferocious who can stand in Satan's face, come sifting or high water, and violently seize the kingdom by force. "And from the days of John the Baptist until now the kingdom of heaven suffereth violence, and the violent take it by force" (Matt. 11:12).

You cannot destroy the works of Satan by lying in bed. If the widow in this parable would have stayed at home, never bothering the judge, she would have remained in her oppressed state. If you're going to get what God's Word has promised you, and that is the ability "not to faint," you're going to have to fight.

Every day we are surrounded by the faithlessness, perversion, hatred, fear, plagues, disease, and the numerous God-haters of the devil's demonic kingdom. In this last day, governments that do not fear God or regard His people will attack our beliefs, but we can stand, unmoved by it all, as we ceaselessly contend from God's dimension in our purpose and will to fight.

Prayer is a heart attitude that will affect our words and actions! Prayer aligns our words and actions with the truth of God's Word and will.

When your attitude is right and the devil seeks to sift you…

You will put on a heavenly mind-set and look to the Potter's wheel, believing for refining, not destruction.

You will stand firm in your cause with bulldog tenacity like the widow, expecting to receive nothing short of vindication because of your guiding truth.

You won't faint.

You will pray always, without ceasing, because every action and word will be focused on God's purpose in your life.

When the fires of Nebuchadnezzar's furnace rage, we lock our wings and let the breath of the Holy Spirit pull us through the temporal situations that present themselves every day. Isaiah prophesies that we shall mount up on eagles' wings when we wait (cling to and abide) on the Lord and that we will run through life's battles with the energy of faith:

> But they that wait upon the LORD shall renew their strength; they shall mount up with wings as eagles; they shall run, and not be weary; and they shall walk, and not faint.
>
> —ISAIAH 40:31

There is no fainting in God's presence. When you study this passage, you find that the pinions and feathers of the eagle represent an escape route for younger Christians and that God will swoop down to deliver His eaglets as they grow up in Him. But God expects His children to grow up. That doesn't mean He won't swoop down to deliver and protect us from certain situations now and then. He does. But those times become fewer and fewer as we mature in Him, because He doesn't want to be our spare tire, so to speak, to make a way of escape from conflict. He wants us to walk through the troop and overcome in the fight.

Our prayer is not to escape but to persevere. When you go through the battle and pray through your trials, you will maintain your purpose and vigilance in Him. As you truly pray, you will be intertwined with God's purpose for your life. You will understand that the Holy Spirit is dwelling inside of you and you will walk through that troop, because "greater is he that is in you, than he that is in the world" (1 John 4:4).

When you are *praying through,* you won't care what your eyes can see when you're praying through your situations and waiting on the Lord. You won't be wringing your hands in fear and fainting at the unrighteousness that abounds. No! You will be praying through with your mind set on those things above, allowing the kingdom of God to reign wherever you are.

PRAYING THROUGH

Without the holy, consecrated understanding of this proper heavenly minded attitude concerning your purpose and everything that happens on any given day, the expression of "praying through" may sound like praying through "to make it to the end one day in the 'sweet by and by.'" But that's not it. *Praying through* simply means "walking through life with our attitudes at God's altitude in the heavenly realm where our minds are continually fixed."

If the reason you get up on any given day is to pay your bills, you will faint when opposition raises its ugly head. When Satan begins to sift, when he calls on his Nebuchadnezzars to threaten you with his fires, you will faint. But when you're going forward in fulfilling the purpose you were created to fulfill, your actions will dictate your actions and words, and God will release His power to see you through to the end. Every action you take, every motivation of the heart, and every prompting of the mouth will have at its core the kingdom of God. You will be vigilant, like the widow in Luke 18, and God will avenge you speedily as you walk in this kind of faith.

God is simply waiting to hear your cry. Jeremiah 33:3 says, "Call unto me, and I will answer thee, and shew thee great and mighty things, which thou knowest not." He is wanting you to declare who Jesus is in your situation. Heavenly minded people call on Jesus' name and declare Him as Lord in their daily affairs to receive His direction and comfort. Those who believe anything that happens on any given day is completely God's will envision Jesus as seated and passively watching, as a inactive, nonparticipant Lord of life. If that were true, He would have never needed to send us the Holy Spirit.

Certainly God is sovereign, and Jesus' work is finished, but our works are the reason He died, to bring others to Him, and they are never finished. So He is ever waiting to hear our cries, to present them to the Father, to release His redemptive power. His Holy Spirit prays and intercedes through us without ceasing.

This is why Jesus teaches that we "ought to pray." This is why Paul taught to "pray without ceasing." With this knowledge, the redemptive promises of God, and the power of the Holy Spirit, we have no excuse to faint. When the fires of God's calling get hot and the enemy of our soul is there to fan the flames as he sifts those around us to attack and defame, it is there, within life's trying flames, that we are forged into champions adequate for the Master's use. It is then that we can stand knowing that God is our deliverer while we give the good testimony of Shadrach, Meshach, and Abednego as the flames of Satan's furnace rage: "If it be so, our God whom we serve is able to deliver us from the burning fiery furnace, and he will deliver us out of thine hand, O king. But if not, be it known unto thee, O king, that we will not serve thy gods, nor worship the golden image which thou hast set up" (Dan. 3:17–18).

As the last day races to its eternal end, we can have confidence that God's will in righteousness, despite what unfriendly governments, employers, neighbors, or school officials say, will win the day as we stand and pray. Sickness, disease, and oppression can't stay when we're armed with this attitude of prayer.

When we are in His will, praying always, and walking out our purpose, there is only seedtime and harvest. I cannot stress enough the importance of what actually comes out of our mouths. If the seed you're planting for harvest is destined to produce the devil's fruit, don't plant it. And don't be running around watching what others say. Just police yourself.

I regularly police myself. Not long ago my wife and I were driving to church. I started to say something about a certain situation that was going on in the ministry, and I caught and cautioned myself, "Now, Rod, is saying what I'm about to say going to produce God's kingdom? If it's not going to produce the kingdom, and the kingdom is His will, then it won't produce His will, and I won't be praying always as I ought." So I didn't say it.

When we agree with what God has promised His church, we can have confidence, come what may, because our confidence is not in ourselves; it is in the power of God's love to redeem us and place us in His will: "And this is the confidence that we have in him, that, if we ask any thing according to his will, he heareth us: and if we know that he hear us, whatsoever we ask, we know that we have the petitions that we desired of him" (1 John 5:14–15).

PRAYING THROUGH CONFORMS US TO CHRIST'S IMAGE

The Bible tells us to live on our Potter's wheel in a constant process of conformity to the image of Christ: "For whom he did foreknow, he also did predestinate to be conformed to the image of his Son, that he might be the firstborn among many brethren" (Rom. 8:28–29).

We are firmly instructed to seek God continually, always, without ceasing, in a heavenly minded attitude of prayer; it is there that the mind of God can touch and renew our vision to go forward and win the day. Vision that is clear, virtue that is right, and victory that is assured is God's vision for His people. And He will help His surrendered people when we cry out for deliverance.

Prayer is the key to conforming into Christ's image when the fires of life threaten to consume our thoughts. It is within those seasons of interaction with our holy Father in the good and troubled times that His loving compassion forms and encourages us in Spirit and in truth. Remember, He has been where we can't go. He is the Alpha and the Omega, the beginning and the end, and He will avenge speedily His elect who cry to Him day and night.

Ask yourself:

- *Have I been crying?*
- *Is there victory in my life?* Has Jesus been on the throne of your life or simply off to the side?
- *Has the unrighteous judge refused my cries for justice?* That parabolic judge can represent the financial, medical, and social systems of this world.

If God's promises to you are being swallowed in the chaos of this last day, take these spiritual steps immediately.

1. Cry out to God in prayer. Open your heart to His Spirit.
2. Cry out in repentance. Deal quickly and thoroughly with sin in your life.
3. Cry out for His purpose and will. Establish His purpose, seeking first His kingdom in your life; lock your wings so that you will soar on the currents of His wind, the Holy Spirit.
4. Cry out for your justice according to God's Word. "He hath shewed thee, O man, what is good; and what doth

the LORD require of thee, but to do justly, and to love mercy, and to walk humbly with thy God?" (Mic. 6:8).

As the final hour before eternity approaches, it will be God's purpose at work in you that gives the strength to soar through every conflict and rise to greater heights. As you pray through your daily situations, your prayer life will resound through your actions and consistent forward motion, undeterred by what you see. And God will use you to help others as they stumble along the way.

In this last day before eternity, we must pray through and walk in supernatural power. Get ready to realize the power of inviting Jesus into every situation of your life.

SEVEN

BIG FAITH
IN A BIG GOD

And he could there do no mighty work, save that he laid his hands
upon a few sick folk, and healed them.

—MARK 6:5

"Hey! Aren't You Jesus, the son of Joseph the carpenter? We know You! What is this nonsense about You? Move along to another place now where You can fool the unsuspecting!"

These were like the words of Jesus' hometown folk in Nazareth when He ministered there almost one year after He launched His ministry. Historians agree that His popularity was immense during the first year of His ministry, but now in Mark 6, at the beginning of year two, His popularity had waned.

Can you imagine that? The popularity of such a miracle-worker in religiously minded Israel, waning in the face of so much agony and need? If you can't, just look out your door. Look in many churches today who receive Him as Savior, but reject Him as anything more.

While the church is God's agent of change, the world may not be interested in changing even if that change means salvation, healing, and restoration. Because the church is revolutionary, the world is threatened by its invasion and resistive to its message. Not only does the world resist the revolutionary, life-changing power of the gospel proclaimed by the church, but you may be resisting God's change in your own life as well.

In this last day before eternity, the world needs life-changing faith in Jesus to be saved. Now, look into your own heart, and ask yourself these questions: *Who is Jesus to me? Is He Savior, Healer, Baptizer in the Holy Spirit, and my coming Lord?*

I asked myself these questions at the foot of my bed as a young man wondering about the reasons of His "inconsistent" work.

THE DESTRUCTIVE POWER OF UNBELIEF

I grew up in church, and I saw one thing in the Bible and another in my church. I struggled for an explanation of the ambivalence among those who said they were believing for healing or other blessings, yet never seemingly received. "Why is that You seem to do so much for some people and none for others, Lord?" was my eager plea.

I had been taught that God was the "Father of lights, with whom is no variableness, neither shadow of turning" (James 1:17). But there was so much "variableness" in which it seemed that He did more for certain ones than others.

I had also been taught that God was no respecter of persons. So I wondered and questioned. And it was Jesus' "failed" ministry in Mark 6 that finally brought my answers.

> And he went out from thence, and came into his own country; and his disciples follow him. And when the sabbath day was come, he began to teach in the synagogue: and many hearing him were astonished, saying, From whence hath this man these things? and what wisdom is this which is given unto him, that even such mighty works are wrought by his hands? Is not this the carpenter, the son of Mary, the brother of James, and Joses, and of Juda, and Simon? And are not his sisters here with us? And they were offended at him.
> —MARK 6:1–3

I could see from this brazen passage that the reason Sister Smith received her healing and Brother Jones didn't was because one accepted the ministry of Jesus and believed for the manifestation; the other didn't. Both said they were believing. Both wanted to receive, but as Jeremiah prophesied, "The heart is deceitful above all things, and desperately wicked: who can know it?" (Jer. 17:9). So what Sister Smith was saying was believed in her heart, but what Brother Jones was saying wasn't.

When Jesus moved into Nazareth to bring salvation and healing to His hometown, few valued and believed His words of truth. They were amazed at His teaching and at the reports of His works, but they were offended and rejected Him in their unbelief.

The word *offended* used in Mark 6:3 is the word from which we get our English word *scandalize*. Therefore, when Jesus brought His ministry to His hometown, we can know that they not only rejected Him, they also scandalized His presence in probably much the same way as they did a year earlier when they tried to throw Him off a cliff (Luke 4:28–30). And the result was powerfully blatant and serves as a reminder to us today:

> But Jesus said unto them, A prophet is not without honour, but in his own country, and among his own kin, and in his own house. And he could there do no mighty work, save that he laid his hands upon a few sick folk, and healed them. And he marvelled because of their unbelief. And he went round about the villages, teaching.
>
> —MARK 6:4–6

Unbelief will stop the power of God in the life of the one who chooses to let unbelief guide them through life.

At Sunday services at the church I pastor, World Harvest Church, God is just as apt to put a brain in the skull of a baby born without one as He is to do anything else. We have seen miracles in our midst that should remove the doubt of any. But it doesn't. Some continue to disbelieve in their need when faith could bring relief.

You may not see any healings or miracles at the church down the street. Why? The heart is greatly deceptive. Doctrines of dispensationalism and what stuck in someone's thinking at one time of his life is a complicated thing that gives the devil a stronghold of resistance. Why the preaching of God's Word and the demonstration of His goodness doesn't remove that blockage for some is a mystery. But is it any more of a mystery than the response Jesus received in Nazareth?

Surely Jesus' supernatural deliverance that day when He walked through their midst at the cliff must have opened a few eyes. And surely the eyewitness accounts and reports of His first year of ministry had reached their ears. But their hearts were hardened, and Jesus "marvelled" because of their unbelief.

How Big Is Your God?

How big is your God? Are you truly a believer? Or do you struggle in unbelief? My denominational background brought me salvation, but I had to move on to receive more of His blessings on my plate. As I progressed in my understanding of God's Word, faith began to build, and Jesus grew in stature in every area of life. Romans 10:17 says, "Faith cometh by hearing, and hearing by the word of God." As I grew from faith to faith, God continually grew bigger and continually assured me, "I will be everything to you that you will allow Me to be." This is why Jesus continued to go "round about the villages, teaching," after He marveled at Nazareth's unbelief.

Teaching destroys unbelief as it produces faith. It is the size of your faith that determines the size of your God. You only need to read the Gospels to witness the power of God's Word to produce miracle-believing faith by looking at the disciples. None of these men had a clue concerning who Jesus really was, let alone what kind of power He had given them. But they believed when they were stirred by His teachings and witnessed His miraculous works. And they believed when they were sent out to do His works. "And the seventy returned again with joy, saying, Lord, even the devils are subject unto us through thy name" (Luke 10:17).

When He raised the widow of Nain's son from the dead, right in the middle of the funeral procession, the disciples were there (Luke 7).

When He fed the five thousand, the disciples served the fish and bread (Matt. 14).

When Jesus cast out the devil from the demoniac at the Gadarenes, the disciples witnessed the change (Matt. 8).

And when He taught them from place to place and around their meal table, His chosen twelve were changed from faith to faith. Yet, even in the midst of all His glory, Judas Iscariot would not believe. Thomas had to put his hands in the nail scars to believe the report that He had risen, even though Jesus announced His resurrection time and time again. So faith is the foundation of our Christian life. *In this last day before eternity, God wants to heal the sick, raise the dead, cast out demons, and work miracles that will astound the unbelieving world.*

When you walk down the street to the local evangelical church, they tell you how to be saved. When you go down to fellowship with some of our Baptist brethren, bring your unsaved relatives and sinners off the street, because no one leaves a good evangelical meeting without hearing the word of salvation and being given an opportunity to be saved. Why? Because Jesus is BIG, faith is BIG, for salvation in the evangelical church. I wouldn't bring too many sick friends there to receive healing or a miracle, though. Why? Because Jesus isn't very big as Healer in evangelical circles.

Pentecostal and charismatic churches have larger faith in this area, but on the other hand, our faith for salvation isn't that big; salvation isn't preached and isn't as big in many of our churches as it is in evangelical circles. It's sad to say, but you probably wouldn't want to bring too many unsaved folks to some of our Holy Ghost baptized services. Why? Because so often we just run on until the end without a word about salvation; then we say a few things and give a salvation invitation at the close of the service. And because faith comes by hearing the Word, the little bit of teaching on salvation toward the end that we do give may not be enough to bring a sinner up front.

Jesus will become everything we allow Him to become in our life, and it is faith that establishes the largeness of His picture. This is why we see Him commending men for great faith, little faith, and no faith throughout the Scriptures.

GREAT FAITH

When the Roman centurion who sought healing for his servant told Jesus to "speak the word only, and my servant shall be healed," Jesus commended him by saying, "I have not found so great faith, no, not in Israel" (Matt. 8:8, 10). Jesus was big enough in the faith of this Gentile commander to believe a simple word spoken could produce the desired result.

LITTLE FAITH

When Peter walked on the water and took his eyes off of Jesus, fixing them on his dangerous situation, Jesus admonished him, "O thou of little faith, wherefore didst thou doubt?" (Matt. 14:31). Peter's faith went from *great* (to move him out of the boat to walking on the water!) to *little* when the situation surrounding him minimized his trust in Jesus.

NO FAITH

When the disciples were crossing the Sea of Galilee with Jesus in the boat, they feared for their lives when a storm arose. Jesus rebuked them, saying, "Why are ye so fearful? How is it that ye have no faith?" (Mark 4:40). It was only a few hours earlier that Jesus had told them they were going over to the other side, but when adverse circumstances arose, the disciples chose to believe what they could see.

When you examine the great ministry built by my mentor and spiritual father Lester Sumrall, you will find the core and breadth of his powerful world outreach wasn't even built until he was fifty years old. Fifty is an age many would fall back, but not Lester Sumrall. Jesus was huge in Dr. Sumrall's vision to believe for a world outreach center with television and radio stations and a world hunger organization that would fly and ship food to the needy around the world. And it was all fulfilled when his former denomination said he was "over the hill."

Jesus has to be huge in most large ministries we ever hear about, or the ministry itself would never have grown huge enough to hear about. We are being blessed and growing because of our faith here at World Harvest Church in Columbus, Ohio. It is great to see Him bless the works of our hands. He knows we don't want hype or fame, so our television station numbers are growing daily and thousands are being touched by the Master's hand. Get this in your spirit: Faith is the key that unlocks the Lord's ability to be what you need Him to be in your own personal life.

When the Lord brought His ministry team to the regions of Caesarea Philippi in Matthew 16, He challenged them to see how big He appeared to them. They had ministered with Him for quite some time by then, they had seen many miracles, and they had worked a few themselves when sent out in pairs. Now Jesus wanted to know where they were in their thinking concerning who He really was.

> When Jesus came into the coasts of Caesarea Philippi, he asked his disciples, saying, Whom do men say that I the Son of man am? And they said, Some say that thou art John the Baptist: some, Elias; and others, Jeremias, or one of the prophets. He saith unto them, But whom say ye that I am? And Simon Peter answered and said, Thou art the Christ, the Son of the living God. And Jesus answered and said unto him, Blessed art thou, Simon Barjona: for flesh and blood hath not revealed it unto thee, but my Father which is in heaven. And I say also unto thee, That thou art Peter, and upon this rock I will build my church; and the gates of hell shall not prevail against it. And I will give unto thee the keys of the kingdom of heaven: and whatsoever thou shalt bind on earth shall be bound in heaven: and whatsoever thou shalt loose on earth shall be loosed in heaven. Then charged he his disciples that they should tell no man that he was Jesus the Christ.
>
> —MATTHEW 16:13–20

Only Peter understood the eternal hugeness of who Jesus really was. The others could only pass along secondhand rumors of His *supposed* identity. And if you're living on secondhand rumors of what your wife, friends, or pastor believe about who Jesus really is, your faith will be little, because hearsay isn't faith.

But Peter knew. Peter understood by revelation from heaven that this Man, for whom he had left houses, mothers, brothers, sisters, and a fishing business, wasn't the transmigrated soul of some dead prophet. And he knew this Man wasn't merely a prophet. This extraordinary being walked on water, raised the dead, cast out demons, healed the sick, turned water to wine, and turned air into bread and fish that Peter personally served and ate. And His words produced great faith in Peter's heart. When the others screamed out "Look! A ghost!" as Jesus approached atop the waves of the Sea of Galilee, Peter responded to Jesus' calming words by saying, "If it is You, tell me to come, and I will!" (See Matthew 14:28.)

Faith is born of the heart. It comes out of your spirit, directs your actions, and speaks out of your mouth. Mental reasoning has nothing to do with it. Therefore, when you say something and then try to disclaim it by saying, "That wasn't me," you're really making a misstatement. As Jesus said, "Out of the abundance of the heart the mouth speaketh" (Matt. 12:34). And we are truly the possessors of our heart. Everyone knows it's just like you to talk the way you do because they've heard you talk that way before!

So, Jesus questioned His disciples in Caesarea Philippi to hear the abundance of their hearts. And He will do that with you today. He will walk right up into the middle of your situation and ask, "Who do you say I am . . . Rod, Joni, Ron, Ashton, Austin?" Then He will stand back to listen, knowing that He will be released to be as big in our lives as our faith will allow Him to be. He's waiting for you now to say who He is so He can step into the arena of your life and become who your faith declares Him to be for you.

If you need salvation, Jesus wants to be your Savior:

> Be it known unto you all, and to all the people of Israel, that by the name of Jesus Christ of Nazareth, whom ye crucified, whom God raised from the dead, even by him doth this man stand here before you whole. This is the stone which was set at nought of you builders, which is become the head of the corner. Neither is there salvation in any other: for there is

none other name under heaven given among men, whereby we must be saved.

—ACTS 4:10–12

If you're struggling with fear in a certain situation, Jesus wants to be your peace:

Peace I leave with you, my peace I give unto you: not as the world giveth, give I unto you. Let not your heart be troubled, neither let it be afraid.

—JOHN 14:27

If you need healing, Jesus wants to be your Healer:

How God anointed Jesus of Nazareth with the Holy Ghost and with power: who went about doing good, and healing all that were oppressed of the devil; for God was with him.

—ACTS 10:38

Jesus Christ the same yesterday, and to day, and for ever.

—HEBREWS 13:8

If you're boiling in the scorching flames of a fiery trial, Jesus wants to be your Deliverer in the furnace:

He answered and said, Lo, I see four men loose, walking in the midst of the fire, and they have no hurt; and the form of the fourth is like the Son of God.

—DANIEL 3:25

If you need financial provision, help in your home life, strength on the job, or faith for greater things, Jesus will be all of these thing to you, as your faith allows Him the opportunity to minister to your life:

But of him are ye in Christ Jesus, who of God is made unto us wisdom, and righteousness, and sanctification, and redemption:

that, according as it is written, He that glorieth, let him glory in the Lord.

—1 CORINTHIANS 1:30–31

Peter knew of his need for Israel's Messiah, and he believed he received Him. So he confessed it, and Jesus changed his name from Simon, "a swaying reed," to Petra, "a rock." And when his sifting was over, Peter became an immovable rock of faith who believed and released into his generation everything Jesus wanted to be.

To be led by faith is to be a person of faith that is absolutely convinced of God's promises, regardless of what we see, feel, or hear. It can be little, large, or not at all. And in these waning hours of church history as we know it, the church is going to need it LARGE. If the Word of God says supernatural signs will accompany our preaching of the gospel, then we should believe it.

> And these signs shall follow them that believe; in my name shall they cast out devils; they shall speak with new tongues; they shall take up serpents; and if they drink any deadly thing, it shall not hurt them; they shall lay hands on the sick, and they shall recover.
>
> —MARK 16:17–18

If the Lord worked with the disciples confirming the Word with signs following it, then we should believe that He will work with us. "So then after the Lord had spoken unto them, he was received up into heaven, and sat on the right hand of God. And they went forth, and preached every where, the Lord working with them, and confirming the word with signs following. Amen" (Mark 16:19–20).

Consider how the Scriptures answer these vital questions for the final hours before eternity:

1. Should we be the ones who determine whether or not Jesus wants to raise the dead?

The Bible says, "But Peter put them all forth, and kneeled down, and prayed; and turning him to the body said, Tabitha, arise. And she opened her eyes: and when she saw Peter, she sat up" (Acts 9:40).

2.   Should we forbid prophecy or speaking in tongues?

The Bible says, "Wherefore, brethren, covet to prophesy, and forbid not to speak with tongues" (1 Cor. 14:39).

What if the woman standing in front of you in the checkout line at the supermarket needs healing from the palsy, and you sense the urge to pray for her healing? Should you grieve the Holy Spirit and disallow God the glory?

What if Jesus wants to heal the man in your office who is dying from AIDS? Should you be the one who disallows giving Him the glory?

Now, I'm not advocating that anyone go out praying for people at random to see who gets what. Jesus didn't do that. In fact, in nine out of ten cases, the sick and those in need came to Him.

In this last day before eternity God wants a revolutionary church that is led by faith and empowered by the Spirit to change the world. What does God want in this last day before eternity?

God wants a church who can be sensitive to those times when He wants to heal, whether that be in the supermarket, at a ball game, or at a post-service altar call at the local church.

God wants a church that sees Him large enough to be their Provider, Healer, Baptizer in the Holy Spirit, and coming King, to the extent that they can release Him along their paths in these powerful redemptive areas wherever they go.

God wants a church of faith, who will invite Him into their midst, without scandal and unbelief, who will simply let Jesus be everything He died to be. "Then touched he their eyes, saying, According to your faith be it unto you" (Matt. 9:29).

God wants a revolutionary church to be His agent and vessel of change in a world desperate for the saving, healing, and delivering power of Jesus Christ!

Will you be such a church in these final hours?

_____

_____

_____

_____

_____

_____

_____

_____

_____

_____

_____

_____

_____

_____

_____

_____

_____

_____

_____

_____

_____

 EIGHT

DON'T DEAL
WITH THE DEVIL

For ye have not received the spirit of bondage again to fear; but ye have received the Spirit of adoption, whereby we cry, Abba, Father.

—ROMANS 8:15

The radically surrendered Christian, shaped on the Potter's wheel, is built in battle, marching victoriously through Satan's sifting and scorching fires of opposition. Walking by faith, we endure with perseverance and hope these final hours of the last day before eternity. For those of us who aren't playing church, we are on a journey to a place called the New Jerusalem, the ultimate Promised Land of God's Holy Word. To get there, we will be changed by the Rapture or resurrection. We will be re-created and restored to the original state of Adam in the Garden of Eden. This is where man started, and this is where he will return eternally, world without end.

I hope by now that you've received the startling picture that the revolutionary church is on a mission to change and transform the kind of prim and proper Sunday-go-to-meeting "churchianity" that we in America have passed off as our mission for some two hundred years. We're on a mission to destroy the works of Satan and to bring as many converts with us into the next stage of mankind's redemption that Bible prophecy calls the millennial kingdom. There, the born-again host of God's saints will live immortally in eternal light.

> For our conversation is in heaven; from whence also we look for the Saviour, the Lord Jesus Christ: Who shall change our vile body, that it may be fashioned like unto his glorious body, according to the working whereby he is able even to subdue all things unto himself.
>
> —PHILIPPIANS 3:20–21

What will Christ's millennial reign be like?

1. In His kingdom, the faithful and obedient church in this life will rule over cities and domains.

> Then came the first, saying, Lord, thy pound hath gained ten pounds. And he said unto him, Well, thou good servant: because thou hast been faithful in a very little, have thou authority over ten cities.
>
> —LUKE 19:16–17

2. In Christ's kingdom, the curse of Adam's sin will be removed from the earth, and Jesus will rule in justice eternally.

> And the LORD will be king over all the earth; in that day the LORD will be the only one, and His name the only one. All the land will be changed into a plain from Geba to Rimmon south of Jerusalem; but Jerusalem will rise and remain on its site from Benjamin's Gate as far as the place of the First Gate to the Corner Gate, and from the Tower of Hananel to the king's wine presses. And people will live in it, and there will be no more curse, for Jerusalem will dwell in security.
>
> —ZECHARIAH 14:9–11, NAS

3. And beyond "there" awaits the renewed fellowship of our Creator Himself, as we look upon His face as Adam once did, without fear of total annihilation from the radiance of His glory:

> And they shall see his face; and his name shall be in their fore-heads.
>
> —Revelation 22:4

> For he looked for a city which hath foundations, whose builder and maker is God.
>
> —Hebrews 11:10

Right now, God's Spirit is changing you into the likeness of what Jesus is now to enter that kingdom as a saint of God. If you're alive at the prescribed date in history, you will be snatched heavenward when the archangel of God sounds his trumpet. Then your spirit will leave your body to be with the Lord and you will receive a new resurrected body, just like Christ's, as you enter those glorious millennial kingdom gates.

There, on that eternal day after the last day before eternity, Jesus will sit enthroned to begin His physical reign on earth. Believe me, you don't want to miss that!

Until Christ Comes—Occupy and Preserve

Until Jesus returns, the revolutionary church has been called to occupy and preserve God's peace in this current age as we wrestle with the powers of darkness to overcome to our glorious end. There is a battle for the souls of men in which we are called to fight. There is a raging war that will either incapacitate Christ's born-again church or militaristically infuriate it to destroy the works of Satan in the neighborhoods, schools, business establishments, and governments of this earth. And the devil doesn't want that.

So Satan prowls around as a roaring lion, seeking whom he may sift and tempt beyond their personal abilities to overcome his powers. But we can be of good cheer! Our High Priest, Jesus

Christ, is praying for us. Do you think He would pray for Peter's faith to become established in the midst of his sifting, and not yours and mine? "And the Lord said, Simon, Simon, behold, Satan hath desired to have you, that he may sift you as wheat: but I have prayed for thee, that thy faith fail not: and when thou art converted, strengthen thy brethren" (Luke 22:31–32).

As we head toward the New Jerusalem with the Lord on that higher plane of life, we are surrounded by devils. But greater is He that is in us, than he that is in the world! Our mission won't be quenched by the prince of darkness. To quote the great reformer Martin Luther: "The Prince of Darkness grim, we tremble not for him; his rage we can endure, for lo, his doom is sure, one little word shall fell him."[1]

The name of Jesus, His Word, and the Holy Spirit's gifts are no match for Satan. So when all is said and done, the enemy has only one recourse—the lie. If the devil can deceive ignorant believers into renouncing their authority in this life, or if he can lie to born-again saints and blind them to their destiny as victors and overcomers in this life, then he can control their lives with fear, guilt, sickness, and disease. And too many of our brothers and sisters in Christ are imprisoned today in his clutches because of buying into his lies.

LET'S MAKE A DEAL

Do you remember *Let's Make a Deal*, the popular game show that aired in the '70s? People from across the nation would appear on it dressed like chickens and soup cans to bargain with the show host to win the big prize. If you were lucky enough to be called on, you would be asked to pick a box, and the trading would begin. If you picked the rusty cheese cutter right away, you were out for the rest of the show. But if your box was at least a year's supply of chewing gum, you could be asked to trade up. And those who lucked out in making better deals could be selected to participate in the big deal at the end of the show, in which they could win a new car, luxury liner world cruise, or some other tantalizing gift.

On this day before eternity, Satan is trying to trick the church with a deal just as Pharaoh, the Old Testament type of Satan, tempted Moses with a deal for Israel. The tempting deals Pharaoh offered Israel parallel the deals Satan uses in attempting to derail the revolutionary church in this day before eternity.

1. Pharaoh offered Israel the deadly deal: *Go and sacrifice, but don't go far.*

Pharaoh was only willing to allow the Israelites to go a short distance—not three days away—and sacrifice to God. But God demanded that His people go on a three-day journey into the wilderness (Exod. 8:27–28). God demanded a radical break with the past, but Pharaoh hoped that Israel would go out and then come back.

Satan's deadly deal for the church: *Go ahead and worship God, but don't leave the past entirely.* Satan tempts us to worship God without personal change. We come to church but go back into the world. We come to the altar and confess, but we return back to sin during the week. We journey to the house of God, but we never become the house of God. If we are to worship God as a revolutionary church, we must leave the past with its sin, traditions, and religion and move into God's radical new thing for our lives. We are the temple of His Spirit (2 Cor. 6:16). Once we are changed, we can never go back to Egypt—sin, religion, and tradition.

2. Pharaoh offered Israel a second deadly deal: *Take your people and your children, but not your flocks and possessions* (Exod. 10:24).

Without their flocks and possessions, Israel could not survive in the wilderness. She would have to return to Egypt after a short journey to sacrifice unto God.

Satan's deadly deal for the church: *You can do whatever you like as long as you stay penniless and powerless.* If Satan cannot keep us lost and bound in sin, he tries to keep the church poor and powerless. He doesn't mind us worshiping God as long as the world sees how poverty-stricken we are. The enemy loves it when shepherds beg for money and sheep rob God of tithes and offerings so that they can just make ends meet at home.

But Israel had her Passover Lamb as do we in order to leave Egypt for good. No longer did she have to look over her shoulder fearing Pharaoh's army, because the army had drowned in the sea. Likewise, Satan and all his legions from hell were defeated at the cross. The only power he has to attack and harass us is the power we cede to him.

Satan knows he can't conquer Christ's church through any power of his own, so he is out to make a deal. He is out to swindle whoever will listen to his shady, twisted pitches. He knows the most heralded funeral service in world history awaits him at the end of the Millennium. And he knows the lake of fire is awaiting all others who will buy into his slick, packaged deals. So, he is daily dealing his deceptions to hoodwink as many people as possible to share his fiery fate.

AND WHAT'S BEHIND CURTAIN NUMBER THREE? HELL!

Hell is what awaits the contestants who let Satan lead them around by the nose to his final three-curtain deal. For the thousands dying every day, there is no universal "God is love and wouldn't send anyone to hell" greeting team waiting behind the curtain to thank and invite them into heaven because of their good works. And there is no reincarnation in eternity. What's hidden behind the curtain is the lower recesses of the grave, the common receptacle of disembodied spirits, which will give up the dead departed spirits at the end of the Millennium to share the lake of fire, or hell, with Satan and his hosts (Luke 16:23; Rev. 20:13–14). The Old Testament calls it the *Sheol;* the New Testament calls it *Hades.*

> And I saw the dead, small and great, stand before God; and the books were opened: and another book was opened, which is the book of life: and the dead were judged out of those things which were written in the books, according to their works. And the sea gave up the dead which were in it; and

death and hell delivered up the dead which were in them: and they were judged every man according to their works. And death and hell were cast into the lake of fire. This is the second death. And whosoever was not found written in the book of life was cast into the lake of fire.

—Revelation 20:12–15

This is what awaits the unbelieving people of the world who buy into Satan's lies of godless religion, humanism, and atheism.

But what of the church? Now I'm not here to split hairs with the once-saved-always-saved doctrines of grace and the traditional church. I won't debate that. But I will say, as I have in previous chapters, that not everything that happens on any given day is orchestrated by heaven to "curse" God's people for training and good. God is sovereign, no doubt about that. And He does what He needs to do despite our best efforts and confessions to the contrary at times. But Satan is alive and well in Christ's ranks, and he is wheeling and dealing out poverty, sickness, and hopelessness every day.

Curtain Number Two: Hopelessness and Despair

This is what Satan's sifting is all about. If he can, he will send a man like Peter, who walked on water *by faith*, into obscurity in a crowd, and he will oppress his mind to the point where he denies any association with Jesus, cowering in fear. If he can, he will kill your pastor with cancer and convince the congregation it was God's will. If he can, he will kill, steal, and destroy from good church members the very last measure of hope through pornography, adultery, divorce, drink, and drugs.

If you don't believe me, just talk to pastors around the nation who will tell you of this one or that one who played "Let's Make a Demonic Deal" with Satan, despite the best efforts of their church. Then read the Lord's stirring parable of the sower in Mark 4 in which He divided His hearers into four distinct groups. Remember? The faith of group one was stolen by Satan immediately: "And these are they by the way side, where the word is sown;

but when they have heard, Satan cometh immediately, and taketh away the word that was sown in their hearts" (v. 15). Group two was robbed later because the seed of God's Word had no root: "And these are they likewise which are sown on stony ground; who, when they have heard the word, immediately receive it with gladness; and have no root in themselves, and so endure but for a time: afterward, when affliction or persecution ariseth for the word's sake, immediately they are offended" (vv. 16–17).

Remember that group three was choked off from receiving God's blessing through the worries and cares that Satan will invariably mix into this life: "And these are they which are sown among thorns; such as hear the word, and the cares of this world, and the deceitfulness of riches, and the lusts of other things entering in, choke the word, and it becometh unfruitful" (vv. 18–19). Group four overcame Satan's attacks to bear lasting, abundant fruit: "And these are they which are sown on good ground; such as hear the word, and receive it, and bring forth fruit, some thirtyfold, some sixty, and some an hundred" (v. 20).

So let there be no mistake about it as we head toward the last day before eternity: This is no time to play "Let's Make a Deal" with the enemy! He is always prowling about, looking to make a deal.

SATAN IS STILL MAKING DEALS

Some misguided preachers say, "Well, the devil's had his teeth pulled, and he can't really do anything." If Satan can't do anything, then answer this:

- Why are the hospitals full and the drug companies and dealers prospering?
- Why are the mental wards and psychiatrists' couches full of patients?
- Why are the school lockers stuffed with pornography, drugs, and guns?
- Why are forty-five hundred babies still being ripped from the wombs of their mothers every day?

And when the liberal and deceived preachers can only answer in muted silence, then I will answer, "Because Satan is the master of the spin-doctoring, phony deal. Listen to him sell: 'Oh, really, Eve? Hath God really said? You know, He knows that the day you finally know about good and evil, you'll be just like Him.'"

"Oh really, Steve . . . Mary . . . Bill . . . Joan? *Hath God really said?* You know, you have a right to be happy on your own terms in this life. So what if that means getting yours before the getting stops being good? So what about your marriage? Everyone's doing it. You have a right to happiness; get that divorce."

"Oh really, Barbara? *Hath God really said?* You know, that group had no right telling you what you could do. You do have more spiritual insight than they do, so break it off. Do your own thing."

"Oh really, Mr. Politician? *Hath God really said?* You know that any sex other than intercourse is not really adultery, immorality, and impurity."

These are just a few of the deal-making pitches Satan bombards the church with every day. Those nurturing in the good, receptive soil of Jesus' parable make no deals, saying, "It is written, Satan!"

Good-ground Eve says, "God put my husband here to dress it and to guard the garden. The Lord commanded him, saying, 'Of every tree of the garden thou mayest freely eat: but of the tree of the knowledge of good and evil, thou shalt not eat of it: for in the day that thou eatest thereof thou shalt surely die.' Now be gone, you snake in the grass, or I'll ask God to make you into a pair of boots!" (See Genesis 2:15–17.)

"It is written! I have put off the old man with his deeds, and I have put on the new man, which is renewed in knowledge after the image of Him that created him. Now be gone, Satan. I will walk my life out in integrity and serve my wife until my days end! I'll have none of your deals. For it is written again, that when He spoiled principalities and powers, Christ made a public display of you, triumphing over you through the cross. And as I resist you, you must flee in Jesus' name!" (See Colossians 3:8–10; 2:15.)

Declare to the enemy, "It is written! I have put aside all bitterness, wrath, anger, clamor, evil speaking, and malice. I am kind to others, tenderhearted, forgiving others, even as God for Christ's sake has forgiven me. So I will submit to those in authority over me, expecting God's will and only good. Pride goeth before a fall, Satan, and I'm not falling for you. So take your little box and game somewhere else, you sleazy game show host!" (See Ephesians 4:31–32.)

Rebuke the enemy with the same words that Jesus used: "It is written, Satan; thou shall worship the Lord only, and Him only shalt thou serve!" (See Matthew 4:10.)

THE FINAL DRAMA OF THE LAST DAY

The final drama of mankind's redemption is about to be played out, and you and I have no time to make a satanic deal. Yet, he is wheeling and dealing everywhere, until we close down his show. So he's roaring around our nation today with rock stars strutting across the stage with nothing more on than a loincloth, making satanic incantations. New Age cartoons still entertain America's children on Saturday morning TV, teaching them the basics of witchcraft. Abortion, greed, and AIDS are reeling our nation. As we enter the new millennium, twenty-five million Americans will be afflicted with full-blown AIDS. In the church, Satan has many of God's people cowering at the sound of his roar through ignorance and religious tradition, which they traded five of his deceptive boxes for on his devious mockery of a show.

Adultery is no longer a sin in Hollywood and in most churches. We need to crush the divorce devil! No more worldly deals! When the Spirit birthed Pentecostalism, the movement that believed in God's supernatural moving that took root at the turn of this century, we preached holiness. We preached holiness when I grew up as a Pentecostal. I heard about separation from the world and a highway out of bondage called holiness.

But today, even the Pentecostals are making deals. God save us! Who wants to make a deal that will torment your soul and send you to hell? Who wants to trade for the goods of this world that will corrupt in eternal places? Who wants to trade eternity for his lies?

LEARN FROM MOSES HOW *NOT* TO MAKE A DEAL

We're currently on a journey to God's spiritual Promised Land of Christ's earthly millennial reign and eternity beyond. And just as he was with Moses' Canaan journey, Satan is here to block your passage to keep you enslaved in Pharaoh's land.

"Let's make a deal," he said to Moses through his servant Pharaoh, "to fulfill your God's will, right here in my land."

> And Pharaoh called for Moses and for Aaron, and said, Go ye, sacrifice to your God in the land. And Moses said, It is not meet so to do; for we shall sacrifice the abomination of the Egyptians to the LORD our God: lo, shall we sacrifice the abomination of the Egyptians before their eyes, and will they not stone us? We will go three days' journey into the wilderness, and sacrifice to the LORD our God, as he shall command us.
>
> —EXODUS 8:25–27

Moses knew there was no fellowship between light and darkness. "No deal, deal maker. Your people won't tolerate our worship," he responded to Pharaoh. "So we've got to go!" But the truth of the matter is, this first deal the devil offered Moses is where so many stumble today.

Beware of the devil's New Age lie: "There's no need for you to pay any attention to those religious Bible-thumpers down the street. You can worship God right where you are with a spirit guide who will show you all the spiritual truth you will ever need. Welcome to the New Age, spiritual seeker! Have a little Buddha, Krishna, and while you're at it, Baal. You don't have to go anywhere. Here, read this book."

And if he can't block passage into the Promised Land of the church, he will entice God's blood-washed family with a little religious sophistication that sounds like this: "You can worship God and live in Egypt. What's wrong with overcharging your customers in business? Grace will cover that. What's wrong with snuggling up to the mind of the world in its sensual music and entertainment?

After all, it's only entertainment." And before you know it, you've traded up to the big curtain deal, and behind it is backslidden drunkenness and immorality.

"Three days away from here ought to be far enough to separate us from your idolatry and evil stench, Pharaoh!" said Moses. "So out we go. No deal, devil!"

But that didn't stop Satan from dealing. So he offered him deal number two:

"And Pharaoh said, I will let you go, that ye may sacrifice to the LORD your God in the wilderness; only ye shall not go very far away" (Exod. 8:28). In other words, "Just go over there to church and sing and dance," said Pharaoh. "Pray your prayers, or whatever you do, then come on back. It's okay to have your religion. I'm not opposed to that. But do you have to make it such a big thing?" And this is the curtain he's traded to so many in the church.

Pastor, you can tell when some of your church members are still shopping in Egypt. You can tell when they're only worshiping on Sundays by how they look and what they wear. Their kids look like something out of a music video. They don't tithe, but they visit the mountain for a little fire insurance.

In other cases it's not so easy to tell when someone has bought into one of Satan's deals. You see them earnestly serving the Lord in insecurity and ambivalence until something breaks in their life, and then you never hear from them again.

But you can know when he's selling you. His thoughts will puff you up and put others around you down. Then he will offer you box number three's strife and division cruise of fellowship separation. And before the deal is sealed, you'll be there in front of his curtains dealing for death, destruction, or hell.

Until that great getting-up morning when we leave this planet to dwell in God's presence on the day after the last day before eternity, it is only our overcoming battles with this fallen angel that will establish God's kingdom in this earth. Until that great getting-up morning, we are called to destroy his works and plant the flag of Jesus wherever we go. We are His only warring agents on this planet, and we're fighting a defeated foe! All he can do is make shady deals. So it's time to say, "NO! No fear! No deal! No!"

For ye have not received the spirit of bondage again to fear; but ye have received the Spirit of adoption, whereby we cry, Abba, Father.

—ROMANS 8:15

The final hour approaches in the last day before eternity. Will you cower in fear and make deals with the devil, or will you march out of Egypt and into Christ's eternal kingdom? Take these life-changing steps now:

Refuse the devil's deal for your life. Don't deal away your marriage, your children, your purity, your faith, or your health.

Rebuke and defeat the devil with the Word of God. Hide God's Word in your heart. Speak His Word of life and not words of death. Exercise your authority to trample on serpents and crush the head of Satan under your feet.

Renew your commitment to your Commander—Jesus Christ. March in His army. Obey only His orders. Establish the kingdom of God by His authority where you live, work, and worship.

Rejoice always, and again I say rejoice! Your God reigns! Never let the enemy steal your joy: "And ye now therefore have sorrow: but I will see you again, and your heart shall rejoice, and your joy no man taketh from you" (John 16:22).

Rejoice! This last day and its final hours are coming to a close. Eternity lies just around the corner. Jesus is coming to take you home. Rejoice!

_____

_____

_____

_____

_____

_____

_____

_____

_____

_____

_____

_____

_____

_____

_____

_____

_____

_____

_____

_____

_____

_____

_____

NINE

HEAVENLY CITIZENSHIP

Since we heard of your faith in Christ Jesus, and of the love which ye have to all the saints, for the hope which is laid up for you in heaven, whereof ye heard before in the word of the truth of the gospel.
—COLOSSIANS 1:4–5

On the day after the last day lies heaven or hell. What awaits you at the end of the last day? Someone once said, "Hell is the absence of reason." Another, "Hell is a state of mind in those of us here on earth." Still another, "Hell is a mythological plane of agony and torment, where injustices are mythologically righted to comfort the innocent now."

None of these statements are right, because none of them are biblical. Jesus talked more about hell than any other doctrine in His Gospel discourses, mentioning the word *Gehenna* twelve times. Why? Because Jesus knew hell was a very real place reserved for Satan and his demonic soldiers, and that men and women deceived by their powers would share their fate in eternal agony. Jesus said, "Then shall he say also unto them on the left hand, Depart from me, ye cursed, into everlasting fire, prepared for the devil and his angels" (Matt. 25:41).

As I mentioned briefly in the last chapter, *Sheol* and *Hades* are the intermediate regions of the damned. This is where the rich man in Jesus' Luke 16 account burned in tormenting agony when he pleaded to warn his family of its coming. Hades, *haides,* or the grave, is the Greek word used in this account (Luke 16:23). But hell isn't populated yet, and it won't be until the devil's Antichrist and false prophet are thrown into its eternal flames.

Why isn't hell populated yet? As I said, the King James expositors translated *hades* as hell in many instances. So to clear up the confusion, another Bible word, *Gehenna,* distinguishes the two regions of the damned.

Hell

Jesus used this word, *Gehenna,* in the Gospels in reference to "the valley of Hinnom," which was a valley to the south of Jerusalem. It was in this valley that the Canaanites worshiped Baal and the fire god Molech with the human sacrifices of their children. Historians say these fires burned continually.

When Jesus walked the earth, the Valley of Hinnom was used as Jerusalem's garbage dump. Its fires burned constantly to consume the refuge and garbage of the city, including the dead bodies of animals and executed criminals. Worms, or maggots, slithered in and out as they bred off of this filth. When the wind changed directions, the foul stench produced by Hinnom's burning would cause residents of the city to cover their eyes and noses.

Because of Gehenna's remarkable stench and purpose, Jesus used Jerusalem's garbage dump to describe the reality of hell. Remember, He always taught the unknown by the known. So He said something like, "Do you want to know what hell is like? If you do, look at the Valley of Gehenna. Remember the refuse of its burning and the stench of its consuming fires. And understand this, the maggots in the eternal regions of the damned won't die, and the flames won't quench."

You don't want to go there, so . . .

If thy hand offend thee, cut it off: it is better for thee to enter

into life maimed, than having two hands to go into hell
[Gehenna], into the fire that never shall be quenched: where
their worm dieth not, and the fire is not quenched. And if thy
foot offend thee, cut it off: it is better for thee to enter halt
into life, than having two feet to be cast into hell *[Gehenna]*,
into the fire that never shall be quenched: where their worm
dieth not, and the fire is not quenched. And if thine eye
offend thee, pluck it out: it is better for thee to enter into the
kingdom of God with one eye, than having two eyes to be cast
into hell *[Gehenna]* fire: where their worm dieth not, and the
fire is not quenched. For every one shall be salted with fire,
and every sacrifice shall be salted with salt.

—MARK 9:43–49

Jesus was teaching prophetically, or symbolically, in this passage
to make the point of the serious nature of sin. Of course, He didn't
mean for anyone to cut off their body parts anymore than He
meant to literally handle poisonous snakes as some misguided con-
gregations literally interpret in Mark 16! When He prophesied that
His followers would handle serpents He meant they would take
care of Satan's demonic hordes, which are typed by serpents
throughout Scripture. So when our Lord painted the picture of cut-
ting off any body part that may send anyone to hell because of the
drive of sin, He meant, "You don't want to go there, even if
avoiding its unbearable eternal damnation would require the sacrifice of an arm, leg, or eye during your time on earth."

Jesus also said that hell would be a place of outer darkness, a furnace of fire, where there will be wailing, weeping, and gnashing of
teeth (Matt. 8:12; 13:42, 50; 22:13; 24:51; 25:30; Luke 13:28).
Revelation describes hell as "a lake of fire burning with brimstone"
(Rev. 19:20; 20:10, 14–15; 21:8) into which the beast and the false
prophet, Satan, and everyone whose names are not found in the
Book of Life will be thrown. The beast and his false prophet will be
hell's first residents at the end of the church age; Satan and those
who will be resurrected out of Hades to face the second death will
then join them at the end of the Millennium (Rev. 20:10–15).

And the sea gave up the dead which were in it, and death and Hades gave up the dead which were in them; and they were judged, every one of them according to their deeds.

—REVELATION 20:13, NAS

And they will be tormented day and night forever and ever.

—REVELATION 20:10, NAS

Surely no one would knowingly desire to be there for eternity.

Hell is a torturous realm of agony reserved for the rebel Satan, who at the end of his spiritual imprisonment during the millennial kingdom will be condemned there along with everyone who collaborated with him not only in this age, but in the age to come. He will be imprisoned, then released at the end of the Millennium, to show how easy it is for the sinful heart of fallen man to be led astray.

I was reading a survey not long ago that said 95 percent of all Americans believe in God; another 50 percent believe in heaven, but only 4 percent believe in hell. It is obvious to me that we don't hear enough good preaching on Hades and hell today.

WHAT IS HELL REALLY LIKE?

Unlike Jesus' parable of the unrighteous judge and widow touched upon in chapter 6, the story of Lazarus and the rich man is a true account. The Bible doesn't announce it as a parallel illustration, and neither does Jesus. Therefore, we receive a powerful glimpse of Hades and Abraham's bosom, or Paradise, as it was before Jesus died on the cross to lead the captives in Paradise heavenward to be with the Lord.

The story involved a rich man who lived a selfish life, including the fact that he didn't reach out to help a poor man by the name of Lazarus, who begged daily at his gates. Both died, both were buried, and both went their separate ways into eternity: the rich man to Hades; the beggar to Paradise.

Now it came about that the poor man died and he was carried

away by the angels to Abraham's bosom; and the rich man also died and was buried. And in Hades he lifted up his eyes, being in torment, and saw Abraham far away, and Lazarus in his bosom. And he cried out and said, "Father Abraham, have mercy on me, and send Lazarus, that he may dip the tip of his finger in water and cool off my tongue; for I am in agony in this flame."

But Abraham said, "Child, remember that during your life you received your good things, and likewise Lazarus bad things; but now he is being comforted here, and you are in agony. And besides all this, between us and you there is a great chasm fixed, in order that those who wish to come over from here to you may not be able, and that none may cross over from there to us."

—LUKE 16:22–26, NAS

What a revelation Jesus allows us in this descriptive passage of the realities of Hades and Abraham's bosom, as it were, before Jesus destroyed the power of death and led captivity captive up to heaven through the cross (Eph. 4:8)!

First of all, we can see from Lazarus' experience that angels carry away the spirit of God's child when physical death releases the inner man. I've heard some personal testimonies to this fact given by some who have visited glory and returned to tell the tale. But we don't really need their testimonies to know this is true, because here, in the Bible, Jesus said it was so.

We can also see that Hades is a place of agony and flame. So the rich man tried to negotiate some relief.

First, he asked if Lazarus could bring him some water. "And he cried out and said, Father Abraham, have mercy on me, and send Lazarus, that he may dip the tip of his finger in water and cool off my tongue; for I am tormented in this flame" (Luke 16:24). Then he sought to warn his family of Hades reality, "lest they also come to this place of torment" (v. 28). But, it was too late.

This powerful worldly figure had no doubt heard the Law and prophets. We know he was Hebrew because he addressed Abraham as "Father," and Abraham reciprocated by calling him "son." And we know there were many righteous Jews who went to Abraham's bosom, or Paradise. But tragically, this man wasn't one of them. Abraham denied his request, reminding the rich man, and everyone who would ever read this story, of the power and accuracy of God's written Word:

> But Abraham said, "They have Moses and the Prophets; let them hear them." But he said, "No, Father Abraham, but if someone goes to them from the dead, they will repent!" But he said to him, "If they do not listen to Moses and the Prophets, neither will they be persuaded if someone rises from the dead."
>
> —LUKE 16:29–31, NAS

Hades, the grave, or Sheol, as it is called in the Old Testament, is very real and awaits the disembodied spirits of those who reject God's favor not only in this age, but in the age to come. There, they agonize with other God-rejecters such as this rich man, to await the Great White Throne Judgment's second death.

> What man can live and not see death? Can he deliver his soul from the power of Sheol? Selah.
>
> —PSALM 89:48, NAS

> And you, Capernaum, will not be exalted to heaven, will you? You will be brought down to Hades! The one who listens to you listens to Me, and the one who rejects you rejects Me; and he who rejects Me rejects the One who sent Me.
>
> —LUKE 10:15–16, NAS

But the born-again saint of God needs to shout and rejoice, knowing that the church of the living God has been redeemed from Hades and hell's second death. Jesus has overcome Hades, and now He holds its keys!

> And when I saw Him, I fell at His feet as a dead man. And He laid His right hand upon me, saying, "Do not be afraid; I am

the first and the last, and the living One; and I was dead, and behold, I am alive forevermore, and I have the keys of death and of Hades.

—REVELATION 1:17–18, NAS

For believers, heaven is our home and destination; it is the home and destination of everyone saved by His grace and given eternal life, which He purchased with His sacrificial blood.

Listen to Peter rejoice when he tells us the family of God has been called to receive "an inheritance incorruptible, and undefiled, and that fadeth not away, reserved in heaven" (1 Pet. 1:4). Listen to Paul's accolades concerning our homecoming to this domain of eternal bliss: "For our citizenship is in heaven, from which also we eagerly wait for a Savior, the Lord Jesus Christ" (Phil. 3:20, NAS). "That in the dispensation of the fulness of times he might gather together in one all things in Christ, both which are in heaven, and which are on earth; even in him" (Eph. 1:10).

This is where Jesus is now, from where He has awaited our homecoming since around A.D. 32. "Who is gone into heaven, and is on the right hand of God; angels and authorities and powers being made subject unto him" (1 Pet. 3:22).

DESIRING HEAVEN AND FORSAKING HELL

So, heaven is waiting. It is our house in which the presence of God will be enjoyed as it was experienced by Adam before his death-defying act opened the portals to hell. This is where every born-again saint longs to be. Like the prodigal son in Jesus' Luke 15 parable, we left our house to go run off to a strange and distant country. When we come to our senses (and it's beyond me why so many don't, choosing to wallow in the pig pen of Satan's filth instead), we crawl out of the pig pen smelling like manure and draw a straight bead for home. Just as the prodigal did, we say, "I will arise and go to my father's house," knowing there is safety, solace, and satisfaction there. And until we get there, until we arrive at heaven's portals to receive our eternal welcome home, we live like our faith father Abraham, as strangers and aliens on this earth.

By faith Abraham, when he was called to go out into a place which he should after receive for an inheritance, obeyed; and he went out, not knowing whither he went. By faith he sojourned in the land of promise, as in a strange country, dwelling in tabernacles with Isaac and Jacob, the heirs with him of the same promise: For he looked for a city which hath foundations, whose builder and maker is God.

—HEBREWS 11:8–10

The writer of Hebrews tells us that by an act of faith, Abraham said *yes* to God's invitation to travel toward an unknown destination that he was to call home. As we discovered in chapter 8, eternity in God's presence as Adam once enjoyed will be the fulfillment of our faith father's sojourn in finding his way all the way home. But it is heaven that awaits as our Promised Land when physical death separates us from our physical bodies or when the Rapture trump is blown.

When Abraham left, he was led by faith and sojourned through life as a stranger, camping in tents. And don't you know Abraham experienced a few siftings, just as we do along our heavenbound trail? Satan sifted him again and again. If you'll remember, he was tempted on the very first leg of his faith journey to fear God's ability to provide for his grocery needs. There was a famine in the land, so he went down to Egypt to survive. Once he arrived, Abram was tempted to lie about Sarai. Fearing for his life, he claimed she was only his sister (Gen. 12). Then he did it again much later in his journey to the king of Gerar (Gen. 20).

So Abraham struck his tents and wandered the earth for twenty-five years until faith arose in his heart to receive his promised son. Twenty-five years may seem long. But it wasn't really to a man who finally died at the ripe old age of one hundred seventy-five. And his forefathering typology is astounding. Addressing the church as "strangers and pilgrims [called to] abstain from fleshly lusts, which war against the soul . . . " (1 Pet. 2:11), the Holy Spirit also typed our human bodies as sojourning tents:

For while we are in this tent, we groan and are burdened,

because we do not wish to be unclothed but to be clothed with our heavenly dwelling, so that what is mortal may be swallowed up by life.

—2 CORINTHIANS 5:4, NIV

Psalm 116:15 says that it is precious in the sight of the Lord when one of His saints experiences physical death because, as Paul continues, to be absent from our mortal bodies is to be present with the Lord.

Now it is God who has made us for this very purpose and has given us the Spirit as a deposit, guaranteeing what is to come. Therefore we are always confident and know that as long as we are at home in the body we are away from the Lord.

—2 CORINTHIANS 5:5–6, NIV

"Paradise" is the word both Jesus and Paul used to describe it, before and after the Lord's resurrection moved it up through heaven's gates. "And Jesus said unto him, Verily I say unto thee, To day shalt thou be with me in paradise" (Luke 23:43).

And I knew such a man, (whether in the body, or out of the body, I cannot tell: God knoweth;) how that he was caught up into paradise, and heard unspeakable words, which it is not lawful for a man to utter.

—2 CORINTHIANS 12:3–4

According to the psalmist, it is a mountain to the north called Zion, filled with beauty and excitement:

Great is the LORD, and greatly to be praised in the city of our God, in the mountain of his holiness. Beautiful for situation, the joy of the whole earth, is mount Zion, on the sides of the north, the city of the great King.

—PSALM 48:1–2

According to Hebrews it is the church's mountain of assembly, surrounded by innumerable angels on which our Father and Jesus await the spirits of men made perfect:

> But ye are come unto mount Sion, and unto the city of the living God, the heavenly Jerusalem, and to an innumerable company of angels, to the general assembly and church of the firstborn, which are written in heaven, and to God the Judge of all, and to the spirits of just men made perfect, and to Jesus the mediator of the new covenant, and to the blood of sprinkling, that speaketh better things than that of Abel.
>
> —HEBREWS 12:22–24

Jesus claimed heaven as home:

> For I came down from heaven, not to do mine own will, but the will of him that sent me.
>
> —JOHN 6:38

Paul decrees it as the place of every true Christian's citizenship:

> For our citizenship is in heaven, from which we also eagerly wait for the Savior, the Lord Jesus Christ.
>
> —PHILIPPIANS 3:20, NKJV

And it is awaiting everyone of us who has earnestly desired to be there and has forsaken hell.

> He that hath an ear, let him hear what the Spirit saith unto the churches; to him that overcometh will I give to eat of the tree of life, which is in the midst of the paradise of God.
>
> —REVELATION 2:7

One day, the church of Jesus Christ will overcome, like the many great heroes of this nation who have responded to war's calling and have fought our enemies to the end. We will be like the American soldier stationed somewhere on the other side of the world who lays down his head to another sleepless night in the midst of a hostile war. Before he closes his eyes, he takes out a crumpled, wet, and torn letter received only days earlier. He has read the letter hundreds of times. But each time he reads it, the words take on new and more significant meaning. Whether it is from his sweetheart, his mother, or from a best friend, the writing penetrates his heart, easing the pain and putting his mind at rest to face one more lonely night.

When the duty-stationed warrior finishes the letter, he folds it and tucks it away for safekeeping until the next letter . . . or the next night. But now he, like us, is ready to endure another day because he knows that this is only a temporary mission—it won't last forever. One day his purpose will be complete, and he will journey home.

Like us, he may be wounded from a battle or two. He may be a little battle-weary. But when he returns home, flags will be waving and crowds cheering as he is greeted with loving, familiar faces.

My fellow prodigals and sojourners, there is a homecoming awaiting everyone upon this earth who has accepted Christ's grace to be skyrocketed heavenward, whether living or dead, that will make every other triumphal procession of a victorious army in history look like a homecoming prom. There will be a triumphant procession and rewards for us sojourners who have been on special assignment for our King. There is going to be a crowning of the faithful who receive Christ's coveted accolade, "Well done, good servant; because you were faithful in a very little, have authority over ten cities" (Luke 19:17, NKJV). The battles we fight before then rage within the invisible realm surrounding us, which we can't see. And our letters from home come from our headquarters in heaven, which dispatches the holy letters of our Commander in Chief, whose words give strength and hope.

Because God has revealed His truth to us, we can face another day in the trenches. Because God has written, we know that when our mission is over, an honorable discharge awaits us, and we know that we have a heavenly home. Whether our orders are cut on that great getting-up day of the coming Rapture or we simply leave our earthly tent to be present with the Lord, our reigning King will be at the gates to meet His faithful warriors and to decorate us as He says, "Company, attention! Well done, thou good and faithful servant; enter into the joy prepared for you before the foundations of the world!"

A VIEW OF HEAVEN

What is heaven? It is that glorious place toward which the revolutionary church of Christ marches. Heaven is being with Christ forever in the eternity that stretches far beyond the final day in which we live.

Heaven has been prepared for the saints. There we will be reunited with all the cloud of witnesses who went on before us (Heb. 12:1–2). In heaven, the Lord—not the sun—will be our light (Rev. 22:5). Heaven is the place of perfect peace (Luke 19:38). Heaven will not have any pain, any tears, or any sickness (Rev. 21:4). Our spiritual bodies in heaven will be in perfect health forever (Rev. 22:2).

Heaven is a place of rejoicing. Mentioned over five hundred fifty times in the Bible, heaven is the dwelling place of the almighty God. It is a place of refuge, a shelter or protection from all danger and distress. D. L. Moody reflected, "The Christian's hope of heaven . . . is not an undiscovered country, and the attractions cannot be compared with anything we know on earth. Perhaps nothing but the shortness of our range of sight keeps us from seeing the celestial gates all open to us, and nothing but the deafness of our ears prevents our hearing the joyful ringing of the bells of heaven. There are constant sounds around us that we cannot hear, and the sky is studded with bright worlds that our eyes have never seen. Little as we know about this bright and radiant land, there are glimpses of its beauty that come to us now and then."[1]

In heaven we will receive our eternal rewards:

- An incorruptible crown (1 Cor. 9:24–25)
- A crown of rejoicing (1 Thess. 2:19)
- A crown of righteousness (2 Tim. 4:8)
- A crown of life (Rev. 2:10)
- A victor's crown (Rev. 4)

Finally, heaven is the place of eternal rest. We will rest from our labor, and our good works will follow us (Rev. 14:13). The wicked will not be able to trouble us, and all who are weary will rest (Job 3:17; Heb. 3:19).

So don't miss heaven! Help everyone you know miss hell, because hell has truly enlarged its borders in these last days on planet earth. The siftings Satan is putting the church and secular world through today are unprecedented. He knows his time is short. But this is all the more reason to get up out of your foxhole, grab your weapon, and double time toward his gates. Jesus said they wouldn't prevail against the church, and that implied a storming, an assault on Hades' halls. So it is time to sign up for combat duty! Turn the page with me and learn how to go to war and win!

> Him that overcometh will I make a pillar in the temple of my God, and he shall go no more out: and I will write upon him the name of my God, and the name of the city of my God, which is new Jerusalem, which cometh down out of heaven from my God: and I will write upon him my new name.
>
> —REVELATION 3:12

TEN

VESSELS
OF REVIVAL

And the dragon was wroth with the woman, and went to make war with the remnant of her seed, which keep the commandments of God, and have the testimony of Jesus Christ.

—REVELATION 12:17

And daily in the temple, and in every house, they ceased not to teach and preach Jesus Christ.

—ACTS 5:42

In this last day before eternity, Christ calls us to radical surrender so that we might learn of His ways and establish His kingdom on earth. The kingdom of God is within us, to destroy the works of Satan as we decimate the devil's attacking hosts of demons with the power of prayer and faith!

The kingdom of God is also above us where God is enthroned and His angels are dispatched to minister to God's people of faith. And, the kingdom of God is beside us, within every saint around us in the body of Christ.

Not everyone sitting next to you in a church service is totally surrendered to Christ. They are like miscarrying trees that bear no fruit. Jesus cursed the barren fig tree (Matt. 21:19ff). We have those in our midst who have had no revelation of Jesus. They bear no fruit, but they pretend to be yielded to Christ. How do we know a fruitful tree? It bears fruit (Ps. 1). Jesus declared:

> I am the true vine, and my Father is the husbandman. Every branch in me that beareth not fruit he taketh away: and every branch that beareth fruit, he purgeth it, that it may bring forth more fruit. Now ye are clean through the word which I have spoken unto you. Abide in me, and I in you. As the branch cannot bear fruit of itself, except it abide in the vine; no more can ye, except ye abide in me. I am the vine, ye are the branches: He that abideth in me, and I in him, the same bringeth forth much fruit: for without me ye can do nothing. If a man abide not in me, he is cast forth as a branch, and is withered; and men gather them, and cast them into the fire, and they are burned.
>
> —JOHN 15:1–6

A tree that isn't miscarrying looks like the early believers. We read, "And daily in the temple, and in every house, they ceased not to teach and preach Jesus Christ" (Acts 5:42). What is the revolutionary church like? It's always bearing fruit; always preaching Jesus; always leading the lost to salvation in Jesus Christ. When you abide in Jesus, you have a continual revelation of Jesus. When someone in the church stops bearing fruit, stops witnessing to Jesus, they have lost their saltiness and are worthless to the body.

When a group of religious folks are fruitless, what do they need? They need to become salty. Jesus calls His church the salt of the earth and the light of the world. We read how salt must be added for healing to come in 2 Kings 2:19–22:

> And the men of the city said unto Elisha, Behold, I pray thee, the situation of this city is pleasant, as my lord seeth: but the water is naught, and the ground barren. And he said, Bring me a new cruse, and put salt therein. And they brought it to him. And he went forth unto the spring of the waters, and

cast the salt in there, and said, Thus saith the LORD, I have healed these waters; there shall not be from thence any more death or barren land. So the waters were healed unto this day, according to the saying of Elisha which he spake.

Out of the revolutionary church of Christ spring living waters that heal a dry and thirsty land. The only way our land will be healed in this day before eternity is for the living waters of God's Spirit to be poured out through believers who are vessels of revival, new life, and living water. Are you bearing fruit? Do you have a revelation of Jesus, never ceasing to preach and teach Him—crucified and raised from the dead?

Some are under constant attack of the enemy and are yielding to his unending temptations. Maybe you've been one of these Christians, and because of this book, you're now ready to serve in God's specially hand-picked remnant who have accepted their call to go all the way! If you are, get ready now to join the ranks of Abraham as sojourning aliens and strangers on this earth. Get ready to walk through the refining fires of life with Shadrach, Meshach and Abednego. Get ready to get out of the boat with Peter. And get ready to heal the sick with John and to cast out demons with Philip!

THE TRUE REMNANT WITHIN THE INSTITUTIONAL CHURCH

God has always had His remnant of faithful followers within the masses of the halfhearted and lukewarm—His church within a church—and that is what this book is all about.

God has always had a people within a people. He has always drawn the heart of a boy, girl, man, or woman from the midst of His people to form them as their Potter, to use them as His vessels in the earth.

When you sense God's draw into His remnant, you will also sense His disdain toward the status quo of church. The emotion-tickling choir numbers, padded pews, and eloquent homilies will lack the depth needed to fill your hunger for discipleship's spiritual quest. Suddenly, the compromising, halfhearted churchianity of days gone by will seem a waste of time as your faith allows Jesus to be your supernatural Lord. And suddenly, you will view those who surround your path on a daily basis as captives to whom Jesus is sending you in wisdom to set free.

Before the Northern Kingdom of Israel was destroyed and scattered throughout the earth, God had His prophetic remnant warn them of their evil, God-rejecting ways. When you read their words in their individual Old Testament books (Hosea, Joel, Obadiah, Jonah, Habbakuk, Nahum, Micah, Haggai, Zechariah, and Malachi), you will hear the heart of every generation's believing remnant as they cry for holiness, fidelity, and justice in the house of God and in the streets.

When the backslidden leaders and masses of Judah's status quo were sent into the captivity of Nebuchadnezzar, Daniel, Shadrach, Meshach, and Abednego were God's remnant people in Babylon to preserve the Jewish race.

When Haman served as Satan's henchman during the Persian Empire to wipe out the Jewish race, Esther was there as God's remnant to destroy the devil's works.

When the time to restore God's kingdom in Israel was ready to be fulfilled, Ezra, Nehemiah, Zadok, Zerubbabel, and thousands of others were there as His trusted remnant to fulfill God's will on earth.

In fact, as you give yourself to the study of Scripture you will find that every book in the Bible was written about and by God's sanctified remnant as a chronicle of God's kingdom business in the earth.

Jesus made a startling declaration: "For many are called, but few are chosen" (Matt. 22:14). When Jesus made this earth-shaking declaration, throngs had been flocking Him, but only twelve knew Him well. Israel at that time had been called. In fact, as you study the Gospels you gradually learn that Jesus' earthly ministry was only to the Jew: "I am not sent but unto the lost sheep of the house of Israel" (Matt. 15:24).

Most of Israel didn't follow Jesus because they rejected His call. "Jesus saith unto them, If ye were Abraham's children, ye would do the works of Abraham. But now ye seek to kill me, a man that hath told you the truth, which I have heard of God: this did not Abraham" (John 8:39–40).

Nevertheless, God has always had a remnant, and He always will: "Even so then at this present time also there is a remnant according to the election of grace" (Rom. 11:5).

Those whom Jesus chooses choose Him in return. This is remnant theology, and it is as old as the story of Adam and Eve's second son, Abel. It was Abel who brought the required blood sacrifice. When Cain murdered him, Eve asked the Lord for a replacement, Seth, who together with his son Enosh brought Jehovah's message of atonement throughout the earth. "And to Seth, to him also there was born a son; and he called his name Enos: then began men to call upon the name of the LORD" (Gen. 4:26).

Moses, Joshua, Caleb, and Rahab make up the famed remnant of Israel's Exodus accounts.

Gideon, Samson, Deborah, and Ruth comprise some of God's remnant during the judges' era.

David, Solomon, Jehoshaphat, Uzziah, and Hezekiah are some of the remnant names made famous during Israel's kingdom era.

Jesus had His church within a church made up of twelve, then extended it to seventy as far as we know. God also had His remnant in the Sanhendrin by the name of Nicodemus and a remnant man in Jerusalem's upper crust by the name of Joseph of Arimethea, who together claimed the body of Jesus and represented Him among their social class.

We see a remnant of one hundred twenty drawn from over five hundred to whom Jesus appeared following His resurrection. These one hundred twenty stayed in Jerusalem in response to His command to wait for God's clothing of power from on high. Where were the other three hundred eighty witnesses? Doesn't it puzzle you why the three hundred eighty didn't wait for Jesus? Why anyone who was privileged to be part of Jesus' post-resurrection seminars and had received Jesus' invitation to be clothed with the power of the Holy Ghost would have ignored the command and opportunity is beyond me.

How many other people actually rejected Jesus' call for whatever reason? We simply don't know. We do see a rich young ruler who rejected Jesus' call. And we see the religious legalists of Israel rejecting His appeals. But God's people within a people have always received Him and willingly reported to duty to get His business done.

The apostle John writes, "But as many as received him, to them gave he power to become the sons of God, even to them that believe on his name: Which were born, not of blood, nor of the will of the flesh, nor of the will of man, but of God" (John 1:12–13). And today, we see God's born-again remnant of sweetly surrendered saints obediently fulfilling the work of God's kingdom . . . while the rest, who have rejected their privilege, watch and stand around.

DON'T JUST STAND THERE; START SERVING!

Standing around watching God's remnant work isn't at all what Paul had in mind when he encouraged the church that after "having done all, to stand" (Eph. 6:13).

No! It is to the remnant that God's power is addressed and through whom He has always shown Himself strong to a lost and dying world. Read Ephesians 6 and arm yourself for battle. Paul wrote, "Stand therefore, having your loins girt about with truth and having on the breastplate of righteousness; and your feet shod with the preparation of the gospel of peace" (Eph. 6:14–15). So, put on the armor of God and stand firm in the battle.

Get on with the business of studying to show yourself approved workmen unto God and soulwinning, Paul tells God's remnant in this passage of Ephesians 6. He is talking to the remnant, because it is only those in God's remnant who obey God's New Testament rules.

"Above all," the apostle continues, "taking the shield of faith, wherewith ye shall be able to quench all the fiery darts of the wicked" (v. 16). Or above all, Paul tells us, be strong in faith to overcome any thought or sifting Satan brings your way!

"And take the helmet of salvation, and the sword of the Spirit, which is the word of God: Praying always with all prayer and supplication in the Spirit, and watching thereunto with all perseverance and supplication for all saints" (vv. 17–18).

Keep your attitude right, the Word tells us, and keep your mind set on God's purpose in life, continually in holy fellowship, while letting God's Word speak!

God's remnant people are called to shine His light into Satan's darkness. We're called to speak His truth into Satan's culture of deceit. We're called to be His peace in the midst of the world's stress and confusions. And we're called to be salt to flavor the world around us while we preserve His truth in the earth.

REJECT THE STATUS QUO

Jesus is continually out to expand His remnant in the earth. So when the religious community in Jerusalem rejected Him because of their legalistic arrogance and deception in the Sanhedren's status quo, He used various symbols in His rebukes to teach the disciples of their error and to save the Pharisees from their ways. In Acts 5, many of the priests did receive the New Covenant truth of Jesus and the sacrifice of His blood. So His many rebukes produced good fruit.

In one instance Jesus called them blind guides, leading the blind: "And if the blind lead the blind, both shall fall into the ditch" (Matt. 15:14).

In another instance He called them "whited sepulchers" to make the point of how outwardly they appeared righteous unto men, "but within [they were] full of hypocrisy and iniquity" (Matt. 23:27–28).

But some of the most powerful symbolic connections Jesus made to the status quo's rejection of His remnant invitation were cloth and wine.

> No man putteth a piece of new cloth unto an old garment, for that which is put in to fill it up taketh from the garment, and the rent is made worse. Neither do men put new wine into old bottles: else the bottles break, and the wine runneth out, and the bottles perish: but they put new wine into new bottles, and both are preserved.
>
> —MATTHEW 9:16–17

In this powerful parable, Jesus painted a picture of how the status quo of mediocrity in religion has never been able to receive the flow of God's truth. He represented God's Word and ways with wine, and the status quo as wine skins, stating that new wine will always cause the old wine in a wine bottle to run out as the hardened structure breaks.

When you see a little group of people start running out of church, you should beware of them, because they are often running out when something new is running in. They leave because they're unable to receive a fresh move, a fresh word, and a fresh anointing. I see it as a pastor. So many come in and become satisfied. But just as soon as they have to make an adjustment of their sails to catch the Spirit's new wind, they hoist anchor and leave, saying, "The wind isn't blowing here anymore. The anointing has left." The new cloth of commitment tears the old cloth of their hearts; the new wine of harvest breaks their old wine bottles, and they are gone.

But not so with the remnant. From faith to faith, to glory to glory, the remnant listen and test by God's Word the winds of change, and then move out in faith to release Jesus in the earth. They are like the faithful saints of old who became examples for today's End-Time remnant:

- Abel brought the required blood sacrifice.
- Seth and Enosh proclaimed God's name throughout the land.
- Noah built the ark.
- Moses forsook his royal surroundings in Egypt and gave mankind God's Word.
- Joshua brought Israel into the land.
- The judges restored the land.
- Samuel established Shiloh.
- David established Jerusalem.
- Elijah destroyed Baal worship in Israel.
- Elisha brought God's Word and power to the people.
- Isaiah and God's many other prophets continued God's Old Testament work while the masses mixed themselves in with the pagan worship of the nations, resisting God's Spirit and heritage on earth.

When in the fullness of time God was ready to institute His New Covenant, it was the remnant to whom the angel Gabriel was sent to announce the good news of the Messiah's coming. Names like Zacharias, Elizabeth, Mary, and Joseph are remnant names! "And they [Zacharias and Elizabeth] were both righteous before God, walking in all the commandments and ordinances of the Lord blameless" (Luke 1:6). "And they came with haste, and found Mary, and Joseph, and the babe lying in a manger" (Luke 2:16).

It was the remnant of Israel, the people within a people, of good honest heart unpolluted by religious arrogance, through whom Jesus established His church in the earth. "And when it was day, he called unto him his disciples: and of them he chose twelve, whom also he named apostles" (Luke 6:13).

And it was Jesus' first-century remnant who would not bow to the terrors of the Caesars in preserving the Word of God for every generation after them:

> Awake, O sword, against my shepherd, and against the man that is my fellow, saith the LORD of hosts: smite the shepherd, and the sheep shall be scattered: and I will turn mine hand upon the little ones. And it shall come to pass, that in all the land, saith the LORD, two parts therein shall be cut off and die; but the third shall be left therein. And I will bring the third part through the fire, and will refine them as silver is refined, and will try them as gold is tried: they shall call on my name, and I will hear them: I will say, It is my people: and they shall say, The LORD is my God.
>
> —ZECHARIAH 13:7–9

Most of Christ's first-century remnant were killed for their faith. Read the Book of Hebrews and *Foxes' Book of Martyrs*. Rome's soldiers would hold a sword to their throat and compel them to deny Christ. When they wouldn't surrender to Satan's temporal cause, they would lose their physical life. Church tradition tells us that John was boiled in oil, but he was supernaturally delivered and banished to Patmos.

BE IMMERSED IN THE RIVER OF GOD

In this last day and these final hours, there's a new move, a fresh touch, a fresh anointing coming to God's remnant today, and it is flowing like a river into holy, remnant hearts. There is always a river on its way from heaven to fill whosoever will with God's anointed presence to establish His kingdom on earth. It flowed to the remnant of one hundred twenty gathered in the upper room while the rest of Jerusalem missed it. It flowed to the remnant in Samaria, Philippi, Ephesus, and wherever the apostles were received.

The river flowed through the Dark Ages and the Middle Ages to preserve God's Word in certain sects that resisted church corruption. Then it flowed on through Martin Luther's reformation doors into the twentieth century through remnant people by the names of Alexander Dowie, Charles Parham, William Seymour, Oral Roberts, Kathryn Kuhlman, Lester Sumrall, and many others. And it is the remnant through whom God is flowing His new wine and power today!

John saw the remnant flow of God's Spirit in one of his last views of eternity in Revelation 22:1 as a pure river of the water of life. So did Ezekiel in chapter 47 of his book as it flowed down from the throne of God to give life and healing to all it touched. It didn't flow from pentecostal denominational headquarters or any other bastion of the status quo! No! It flowed from heaven to a depth that covered Ezekiel's ankles before flowing up to cover his knees and loins. Then it finally swelled into a submerging river with tree-lined banks that Ezekiel couldn't ford.

> And by the river upon the bank thereof, on this side and on that side, shall grow all trees for meat, whose leaf shall not fade, neither shall the fruit thereof be consumed: it shall bring forth new fruit according to his months, because their waters they issued out of the sanctuary: and the fruit thereof shall be for meat, and the leaf thereof for medicine.
>
> —EZEKIEL 47:12

The trees Ezekiel saw, I believe, were typical of us—God's

willing, obedient remnant through whom His river always flows. They were firmly planted next to the river and had healing hands that were typed by leaves, because it has always been God's remnant people who have served as His vessels of healing and truth.

We see this river flowing again to the remnant of Israel in Acts 2. From there it flowed to Samaria, then to the uttermost parts of the earth. We see them laying hands on the sick and casting out devils in the Book of Acts. So it is the remnant—not everybody—but those in the remnant of God who have always laid hands on the sick to bring healing to the nations. They are the ones who have preached salvation and ministered to the poor, who can receive the new wind of His purpose because of softened, open hearts.

God's flowing river bursts out of old containers because of the hardness that sets into the vessels of the traditional status quo. But it is the substance contained within God's bottle, not the bottle that determines God's remnant. For example, I remember when I first entered the ministry, I found this bottle. It was big, tall, and wide. It was so wide you couldn't get your hands around it in the center, but it narrowed toward the top where it had a lid. When I found it, it had the label of a major alcoholic distributorship on it. So I brought it home. I was told, "You can't bring that thing into this house! That's an evil bottle!"

I said, "It won't be when I get finished with it." I washed off the old label, cleaned it up, and set it up in the front room. "Still looks like a wine bottle to us, Rod!" came the criticisms of all who saw it. But then my father and my little three-year-old niece began dropping our first ever Easter resurrection seed offering into that bottle, and it wasn't long before the whole family followed suit. In several weeks, that big old bottle was overflowing. We took it to the bank to get all the coins rolled, and we found out that we had put six hundred dollars for the work of the Lord in that former booze bottle! The old thing that had probably gotten someone drunk, and possibly even put them in jail, was suddenly being used to store six hundred dollars for the salvation and healing of the nations. Before long, everyone in the church wanted one just like it.

Now the point of this story is this: Any organization becomes evil or good based on what you put in it. It is the remnant, not the masses, who allow the flow of God's change for good. And it is the pure in heart who will see God (Matt. 5:8), whether they wear robes or not. This is why Paul wrote that in every house there are vessels unto honor and vessels unto dishonor. "If a man therefore purge himself from these, he shall be a vessel unto honour, sanctified, and meet for the master's use, and prepared unto every good work" (2 Tim. 2:21).

GET READY FOR SATAN'S ATTACK

Finally, it is God's remnant that Satan targets. We are first on his "hit list." Why? Because he has no fear of defeat from the status quo. The status quo is the status quo because he has convinced them to abide by his plan of spiritual apathy and worldly standards. So Satan comes to persecute and sift those who have declared war on his kingdom.

Satan will tempt to distract the hearts of God's chosen few. He will prop up situations and stoke the fires of his servant's ovens in an attempt to stop the remnant's forward motion. But he can't stop us—because fear and vain imaginations are his only fuel!

For each of us, life is an opportunity to rescue from loss (redeem) the days, hours, and minutes of our gift of time. And it is only God's faithful remnant who completely understand this. We know our purpose, so we have reported to the Potter's wheel to be formed and used as He sees fit, "redeeming the time, because the days are evil" (Eph. 5:16).

It is only the remnant of God that truly understand the kingdom of God is living within us to destroy the works of Satan.

It is only the remnant of God who truly understand that because our citizenship is in heaven, we are strangers and pilgrims on earth.

It is the last day.

The final hour approaches.

A remnant church marches through deserts bringing a river of water into a dry and thirsty world.

The revolutionary, remnant church refuses to maintain the status quo. Like a mighty army marching under Christ's banner, she goes forth into battle knowing that victory already belongs to her.

Like a bride marching down the aisle to her husband, the remnant, revolutionary church is marching through the last day with her eyes fixed on only one goal—meeting her Bridegroom at the marriage feast of the Lamb. Ask yourself:

Am I marching with the remnant?
Are my eyes fixed on the Lamb?
Am I filled with new wine?
Am I directed by the new, fresh wind of the Spirit?
Am I ready for war?

ELEVEN

FILLED WITH
NEW WINE

But new wine must be put into new bottles; and both are preserved. No man also having drunk old wine straightway desireth new: for he saith, The old is better.

—LUKE 5:38–39

"Do as the man says, for heavens sake!" shouted the headwaiter nervously as he raced over to where the water pots could be seen in the courtyard's eastern corner. "There are many more wedding guests here than I was originally made to understand, so it's not my fault that the wine has run out. If this man can do what His mother says, we will let Him do it," the waiter continued as he waved to those serving under him to follow him in haste.

"Now we will see," said the bridegroom's father to his wife. "I have heard many things about Mary's prophet. Now we will see."

Once the headwaiter's staff had carried the six water pots to the center serving area at the feast, a small crowd gathered to see what Mary's son would do next.

"Fill the water pots with water!" the strange mystic instructed. The headwaiter directed his servants to form a line from the main cistern, and they started passing water pitchers as fast as they could.

"Fill them to the brim! Everyone of them!" Jesus continued, and as they did, the water changed color the second it left the water pitcher's lip.

"God of Abraham, Isaac, and Jacob," whispered the bridegroom's father to his equally intrigued wife. "Do you see what I see, beloved?"

"Yes," responded his astonished wife. "The water turns red as it pours from the pitchers," she said.

"It turns to new wine," broke in Mary from behind. "It turns to new wine to properly celebrate your children's day."

"Yes, Mary. We see. You are certainly the mother of a prophet . . . yes quite," replied the father, now half-dazed from the sight.

"Draw some out and take it to the master of the feast," Jesus now warmly invited. When the master of the feast had tasted the water that was made wine, and he did not know where it came from (but the servants who had drawn the water knew), the master of the feast called the bridegroom. He told him, "Every man at the beginning sets out the good wine, and when the guests have well drunk, then the inferior. You have kept the good wine until now!"

Water into wine! What an odd miracle to launch the Messiah's supernatural ministry. It wasn't planned by Him, at least so far as we know in Scripture. But its significance is remarkable. Mary, Jesus, and His entire ministry team had been invited to the wedding in the Galilean city of Cana. We don't know the couple who was married. But that's not important anyway, because the significance I want to point out is that two were becoming one, and new wine was a factor.

As I pointed out in the last chapter, new wine is always a factor in the supernatural process of birthing dead spirits back into the likeness of God. That is what we are before repenting of our sin in surrender to God: dead, dark, empty, hardened bottles. But then the light of God dawns in our hearts and His Spirit moves in to give back His abundant life. It is left up to us to allow God's healing oil to continually rub into us to keep us tender and salty. There was great joy at the Cana wedding as a new union began, just as there is great joy in our marriage to Jesus when the new wine of

His Holy Spirit is allowed to continually flow.

New wine, or unfermented wine, and fermented wine were the most common of drinks in Judea at the time Jesus gave this teaching. And both had to be poured into flexible wineskins that were used over and over again.

In Jesus' parable of the Good Samaritan, the Samaritan poured both wine and oil into the robbery victim's wounds, showing the healing properties of both (Luke 10:33–34). We see in the Old Testament there was fermented wine, which brought a happiness of heart; this wine was often connected as a drink offering in the Levitical sacrifices (*yayin*, Num. 15:4–5). And there was new wine that was often connected to the harvest and the tithe (*teeroshe'*, Deut. 14:23).

The fact that Jesus willingly agreed to produce new wine at the wedding in Cana showed God's sanctioning of marriage when He miraculously created wine, which is a type of the infilling joy in the Holy Spirit that happens when we are united with Christ. Like the butterfly, oil and wine are something other than what they become before they are changed. Oil comes from the olive, wine from the grape.

There were no commandments that forbid the Old Testament Hebrew laymen from drinking fermented wine. But there were strict injunctions against imbibing fermented grape juice for the priesthood when they went into the tabernacle or temple to minister:

> And the LORD spake unto Aaron, saying, Do not drink wine nor strong drink, thou, nor thy sons with thee, when ye go into the tabernacle of the congregation, lest ye die: it shall be a statute for ever throughout your generations: and that ye may put difference between holy and unholy, and between unclean and clean.
>
> —LEVITICUS 10:8–10

The sanctified servant of Jehovah, the Nazarite, wasn't even allowed to eat the skin of grape during the period of separation:

> He shall separate himself from wine and strong drink, and

shall drink no vinegar of wine, or vinegar of strong drink, neither shall he drink any liquor of grapes, nor eat moist grapes,
or dried. All the days of his separation shall he eat nothing
that is made of the vine tree, from the kernels even to the
husk.

—NUMBERS 6:3–4

The wisdom of God in Proverbs echoes over and over again the
dangers of alcohol consumption because of its destructive properties. "Wine is a mocker, strong drink is raging: and whosoever is
deceived thereby is not wise" (Prov. 20:1).

I disagree with the theology that teaches moderation and
wisdom in not being a stumbling block to those who disagree with
drinking. Why? Because today, our bodies are temples of the Holy
Spirit, and our calling is to a higher priesthood than Aaron and his
descendants received. Peter says that we are "a chosen generation, a
royal priesthood, an holy nation, a peculiar people; that ye should
shew forth the praises of him who hath called you out of darkness
into his marvellous light" (1 Pet. 2:9).

WINE—TYPE OF THE HOLY SPIRIT

Wine was only a type of the true joy and peace the Holy Spirit now
gives the church. Today, the Holy Spirit is the only joy we need. If
you have been blessed with His presence, you know that being
drunk in the Spirit is being filled with joy and led by His wisdom.
When Christ fills you with the wine of the Spirit, He uses you as a
conduit of His explosive power to work a miracle, heal the sick, cast
out devils, and comfort the mourning.

We can see how wine and union are inseparable types again in
the prophetic type of communion when the fruit of the vine and
bread of life consumed together represent our union with Christ.

And he took the cup, and gave thanks, and gave it to them,
saying, Drink ye all of it; for this is my blood of the new testament, which is shed for many for the remission of sins.

—MATTHEW 26:27–28

The Holy Spirit, the new wine of God, is always doing something new! It may not be new to Him, but it is always new to us, because we are growing up into Jesus from faith to faith in discovering what He always knew. Those who resist His newness and refuse to grow tear as an old garment when a new patch is sown on. They burst like an old wineskin that has been hardened because of a lack of kneading oil worked into the bottle to keep it soft.

It will only be the flexible and soft-hearted who will be able to receive the Holy Spirit's final move in these last days that are racing toward the end of this age. Programmed religion will miss God's newness because the status quo of self-serving humanism stands stiff as hardened wineskins.

In this last day, there is coming a move of the Holy Ghost before the Rapture of the church that will eclipse every other move in history. I believe this book is just one contributing factor in God's overarching plan of remnant preparation for this rapidly approaching day. And if our inner man isn't being renewed day by day, our mind and heart will harden to these purposes and plans.

DRINK NEW WINE

Drinking the new wine of God's revelation is what brought the current charismatic move of God into existence. When Charles Parham and William Seymour allowed the Holy Spirit to pour His new wine into them, the 1906 Azusa Street revivals provided the womb for the new birth of the Holy Spirit's miraculous power in our twentieth century. Azusa gave birth to the healing revivals that shook America in the middle of this century. Those new moves (to us, not Him) gave birth to the Charismatic Renewal in the 1960s that we are still experiencing. And today, God desires to pour new wine into the vessels that were birthed in this past movement to do new thing.

God is calling us to put down our Tinkertoys and the selfish humanism that has swallowed the power of His Word in our selfish pursuits. He is wanting to replace our church motto of "me, my four, and no more" with "Tell me what to do; tell me what to do. I'm through playing, Lord; I'm ready to serve you."

God is looking to increase His remnant, and He is looking to increase it through you. Any ordinary vessel will do, because He makes extraordinary the ordinary that we bring to Him. This is why Paul said in 1 Corinthians 1:26, "For ye see your calling, brethren, how that not many wise men after the flesh, not many mighty, not many noble, are called." Why? So no flesh may glory.

> God hath chosen the foolish things of the world to confound
> the wise; and God hath chosen the weak things of the world
> to confound the things which are mighty; and base things of
> the world, and things which are despised, hath God chosen,
> yea, and things which are not, to bring to nought things that
> are: *That no flesh should glory in his presence.*
> —1 CORINTHIANS 1:27–29, EMPHASIS ADDED

God is looking for those still caught in sin and bondage, and He is looking to set millions free from the "priestly" status quo. There is a new wine flowing from heaven that is changing the hearts of people into vessels fit for noble use, because of who is filling them. I've seen many, myself included, become spiritually intoxicated by the Spirit's flow. I've been in services when the Spirit's presence was so explosive that everyone I laid hands on lost consciousness as they folded to the floor.

There is a growing remnant among us who are saying, "I refuse to participate in churchianity pettiness. I want more of God's Word and Spirit and less of me. I am tired of squabbling with those around me. I'm setting my jaw like flint, and I am walking toward victory!"

I myself have so opened my ministry to the newness of God's spiritual wine that some look at me as if I'm crazy. Sometimes I even feel as if I'm crazy, so I tell myself to be quiet. Lawyers try to shut me up. Devils try to shut me up. It feels like a burning in my bones. But I've got to shout. I've got to praise, because there is a burning in my bones that comes from new wine.

Buildings aren't the answer. The bottle has no cure for what ails us or our surrounding hellbent world. We thought that growth was a sign of receiving God's new wine. Because people filled our sanctuaries, we've thought the Father was increasing and building His kingdom. But we've found out that we're nothing more than status quo, "bless me" clubs, entertainment centers built for a fast-food generation. It is the new wine that fills God's bottle that mends and heals—not the bottle, not the brick and mortar—but the move of the Holy Spirit's compassion and flow.

New wine is for new wineskins that are softened in the heart. Therefore, even though God does choose us ordinary vessels, no mediocrity will do. No old vessel will do. The cracking skins of old bottles can't hold the love, joy, peace, and power God is pouring out today.

There are new works and ministries ahead that the new wine of God's Spirit is wanting to birth. So He is calling and increasing His remnant. He is calling us to press on with Him into the room of Jairus's daughter where He raises the dead. He is wanting our sweet fellowship on His Mount of Transfiguration where the voice of our Father reminds us of who He is. He is forging in the flames of persecution and on His potter's wheel of faith a Holy Ghost equipped army the likes of which Satan's kingdom has never seen.

On the day of Pentecost when those assembled for the great feast in Jerusalem thought the disciples were drunk on new wine (Acts 2:13), so it will be again and again in this last day before eternity. As it was when Philip, Peter, and John brought the new wind of God's outpouring into the city of Samaria and great joy filled the city as the people with one accord gave heed unto those things seeing the miracles, so it will be again (Acts 8). As it was in Ephesus when the power of God inspired the city residents to bring their idolatrous books and objects of witchcraft to the city square, so it will be again (Acts 19).

But it will only be so where humble vessels are open to receiving God's new flow. "For these are not drunken, as ye suppose, seeing it is but the third hour of the day," said Peter on the day the harvest feast of Pentecost was spiritually fulfilled (Acts 2:15).

Joel saw the last days army God is raising up that will follow Christ to the plains of Megiddo to deal Satan's kingdom its final premillennial blow: "They shall run like mighty men; they shall climb the wall like men of war; and they shall march every one on his ways, and they shall not break their ranks" (Joel 2:7).

JESUS WANTS YOU!

God is calling you. God is calling you to be refined in His fires of battle-forging hardness. He is looking for a few good women and men. Imagine with me that old U. S. government recruitment posters on which our stately Uncle Sam, clad in red, white, and blue, pointed a patriotic finger at the poster's onlookers, saying, "Uncle Sam Wants You!"

Now imagine Jesus on that same poster, pointing a compassionate, powerful finger outward, commanding, "The Kingdom of God Wants You!"

At this very moment, the final days of history are ticking off before us, and there is a growing hunger stirring in the hearts of those in whom God wants to flow. The days are growing shorter and shorter, and the kingdom of God wants you! There is a stirring and uneasiness in the old wine bottles that are resisting the Spirit's flow. If you've felt this stirring, check yourself. Get down on your knees right now and pray, "Here's my cup, Lord; fill me up, Lord; fill me up to overflow."

Learn a lesson from Jesus' parable of the ten virgins: Seek to fill your lamp before it's too late (Matt. 25:1–13). Take a lesson from Jesus' parable of the woman who lost her coin, spent all night sweeping her house and looking for it, and then went out to share her joy in finding it with everyone she knew (Luke 15:8–9). Be looking for sweeping changes in your life. If you're sensing a new thirst now as we head into the last chapters of this Holy Ghost handbook, look up and tank up in the Spirit's new wine flow.

Not long after Elisha started walking in the footsteps of his mentor Elijah, certain men of Jericho came to him with a problem: Their water was bad, and their land was unfruitful. So Elisha worked yet another prophetic type.

> And he said, Bring me a new cruse, and put salt therein. And they brought it to him. And he went forth unto the spring of the waters, and cast the salt in there, and said, Thus saith the

LORD, I have healed these waters; there shall not be from thence any more death or barren land. So the waters were healed unto this day, according to the saying of Elisha which he spake.

—2 KINGS 2:20–22

IS THE INSTITUTIONAL CHURCH BECOMING A CULT?

I believe we see another type of the remnant of God's people in this water-cleansing miracle. The bottle is typical of our body, and the salt of God's Spirit. But if we aren't being renewed and preserved in our inward man day by day as Paul admonishes us in 2 Corinthians 4:16, we will lose our saltiness, and as Jesus said, be good for nothing more than throwing out (Luke 14:35). Therefore, Jesus said, "Have salt in yourselves, and have peace one with another." (Mark 9:50). So we need new wine and salt to walk full in God today.

I'll say this until someone listens: We've got all the machinery. We've got the largest, most illustrious church buildings America has ever seen. But many of us are missing out on the only important thing: God's flow. Many of our charismatic brethren have traded in the banner of truth for a humanistic gospel of self-help. Prosperity and success seminars are being held in the place of needed outreach training, and the resemblance of their gatherings look more like an upper-level multimarketing plan than a New Testament church.

I've made this statement over and over again in my Columbus congregation and on television airwaves. So now, read it here in this timely book: *Christianity as a whole today is as cultish as the Jehovah's Witnesses and Mormons.*

How can this be? Because we, like the Mormons and Jehovah's Witnesses, have adopted a form of godliness, while denying the power of God. We have denied God's new wine.

In some charismatic circles we even have a prophet of the week coming in to lie about this or that to manipulate our actions and finances. Many of our people are sneaking around with a wine bottle under their coat and a *Playboy* magazine hidden in a sack, and these so-called prophets tell them how blessed they're going to be. They say, "Yea verily, thine business shalt be blessed." And, "It may look dark now, but things will soon change for the better because you are blessed!" You don't ever hear these false prophets rebuke God's people for robbing from Him because of withholding their tithes, or exposing the corrupt, misled direction of this one or that. Why? Because that doesn't draw a crowd. That doesn't draw a big offering.

In other circles, church has become nothing more than a social outlet. Why? They aren't drinking new wine. They got stuck in the middle of the last outpouring and set up merchandise tables in the tabernacle. But God is calling them to repent and start again!

DRINK GOD'S NEW WINE

Jesus came to earth to bring God's newness to the earth. Moses experienced the new wine of God's glory on the mount. Joshua experienced God's flow in the land. But the people got caught in the ways of the world, and Israel's bottle grew bitter and old. So God raised up judges, and every time the people repented, they drank and were restored to their land. When the kingdom in Israel was finally established, the new wine of God's glory waned after forty short years of glory, but God always had His remnant.

Just read through 1 and 2 Kings to learn who God's heavy-hitter new wine drinkers were. Good kings such as Jehoshaphat, Uzziah, Jotham, and Hezekiah maintained God's righteous remnant because of continually drinking from His heavenly flow. Shadrach, Meshach, and Abednego drank in the midst of Nebuchadnezzar's flames. Daniel stayed on his knees to drink to keep the light that would some day lead God's people home. Ezra and Nehemiah rebuilt the city. In the New Testament, Joseph, Mary, Elizabeth, and Zacharias were ready and waiting when the time arrived for Messiah because of their taste for spiritual wine and an unshakable faith.

As the final hour ticks down, it is almost time for Messiah to come again. And He is coming again to His remnant. He is coming to you. He is coming to me. Thank God for the anointed new wine that is flowing today into humble vessels, sanctified for noble use. Thank God for His mercy and grace that is washing us out of our charismatic playpens into the evangelistic powerhouse of His remnant grace!

Today, Jesus is saying again, "Fill the water pots with water! Fill them to the brim! Fill everyone of them with My Father's new wine! Put it in softened new wine bottles so both are preserved; 'else the bottles break, and the wine runneth out, and the bottles perish'" (Matt. 9:17).

Jesus is busy pouring and filling His remnant, revolutionary church with new wine. He is busy pouring Himself into vessels who will represent Him as Daniel did in Nebuchadnezzar's court. He is looking to fill the few who will go with him into the rooms of Jairus's daughter to raise them from the dead. He is busy filling His vessels who will pray with Him on the mount. He is busy making union in the joy of His spiritual wine, because tomorrow He will be receiving into eternal habitations only those who partake of His fruit of the vine. Obey the command of God to be filled with the new wine of the Spirit:

> Wherefore be ye not unwise, but understanding what the will of the Lord is. And be not drunk with wine, wherein is excess; but be filled with the Spirit; speaking to yourselves in psalms and hymns and spiritual songs, singing and making melody in your heart to the Lord.
>
> —EPHESIANS 5:17–19

In the final hours of this last day, drink your fill of God's new wine. Become intoxicated with the richness and fullness of Jesus Christ. Refuse to drink of the polluted waters of this age, for a new age is about to dawn in which there will be no sunset or dawn. It will be the age in which the light burning within us will be the light that baths the new Jerusalem in eternal day.

The night cannot overcome the light. Shine forth. Be salt and light. As the twelfth hour approaches tend your lamp, preserve your fervor, and blaze forth in passionate witness to the Bridegroom who stands waiting for you to rush into His outstretched arms.

TWELVE

THE FINAL
AWAKENING

*Then began he to curse and to swear, saying, I know not the man.
And immediately the cock crew. And Peter remembered the word
of Jesus, which said unto him, Before the cock crow, thou shalt
deny me thrice. And he went out, and wept bitterly.*

—MATTHEW 26:74–75

The flames of the courtyard fire flickered bright and warm, casting
ghostly shadows on the temple walls that enclosed scattered circles
of people warming themselves. Peter cupped his hands and blew
into his palms to warm himself again.

To the east of this little party's gathering, the Sanhedrin was con-
vening behind thirty-foot cedar doors with Peter's spiritual mentor
and leader, Jesus of Nazareth, as the issue of their late-night
quorum.

"You're one of them; you too were with Jesus of Nazareth," said
the fourteen-year-old girl who had been peering at Peter since he
sat down.

"No, I'm not; I don't know what you're talking about!" argued
Peter.

"But you look like him; I mean, you look like one I saw many times close by Jesus' side, and you speak in their tongue," said the girl as Peter sprung to his feet and began walking toward the temple gate.

"This man was with Jesus of Nazareth!" shouted another servant girl as Peter stepped quickly toward the gate.

"I tell you I don't know the man!" Peter shouted to those surrounding the girl. Then the frightened apostle moved back into the brisk night toward the courtyard's corner to stay out of his accuser's view.

But his tormenting silence was quickly broken by the clatter of footsteps and a booming voice that shouted, "Certainly you are one of them! Your voice gives you away, and many recognize you!"

"I swear to you on the heads of my forefathers that I don't know this man! I have no idea what you're talking about!" Peter cried in one last defense. Then, from beyond the courtyard he heard the crow of a rooster, and Peter despondently fled.

You know the story; it is as much a part of the Gospel narratives as the resurrection of Jesus Christ. Here is Peter, God's chosen remnant man within His remnant, trying to blend back in with the world because of Satan's sifting lies. We know that the great apostle overcame after Jesus appeared to him with many consoling words. But if it could happen to Peter, it could happen to anyone. It could happen to you, and it may have already. The devil will move to block your forward motion, and if he can get you sitting in the courtyard, hopeless and in fear, he has fulfilled his evil work.

This has happened over and over again throughout history as God's people fell asleep and simply blended into the world's system to warm themselves by Satan's fires. It took Martin Luther to wake up the church, moving God's people into a reformation. Many have followed behind him to keep us out of the world's deceptive bed.

In the last eleven chapters I have poured out my heart to allow you to hear God's heart on the spiritual realities of our day. I've done my best to thwart the blending move of intellectual humanism that has infiltrated the church. I've sought to shed some light on the struggles Christians encounter for taking a stand of faith and on the importance of character development on the Potter's wheel.

I've painted a clear picture of how the deal-maker, Satan, will attempt to distract God's people, to destroy them bit by bit through compromise. And I believe I've pointed out the importance of "Plan A Only," a 100 percent commitment on the part of God's redeemed community if His inner-circle remnant are to ever overcome. The common thread that has been woven throughout each of these practical aspects has been purpose: the purpose each unique born-again human being receives when God forms us on His wheel.

The church is currently racing toward our promised heavenward snatching we have come to call the Rapture. We have one more harvest season, one more pentecostal fulfillment getting ready to visit earth before that happens. History is racing toward this outpouring's coming, and earth's fields are ripe for harvest; to harvest those fields, He will need a trustworthy remnant.

WHERE IS THE REMNANT?

It will be the remnant of the church—not all of Jerusalem, but the one hundred twenty gathered in excited anticipation of what the Lord has promised—who will receive the church's End-Time outpouring that is soon to hit this earth. There is no time left for second best. The chaff is being burned, a separation is currently taking place, and God is calling you.

The prophet Joel prophesied the new wine outpouring of the Holy Spirit's coming in his 800 B.C. prophecy:

> I will pour out my spirit upon all flesh; and your sons and your daughters shall prophesy, your old men shall dream dreams, your young men shall see visions: And also upon the servants and upon the handmaids in those days will I pour out my spirit.
>
> —JOEL 2:28–29

Peter announced its fulfillment in his sermon on the day of Pentecost:

> But this is that which was spoken by the prophet Joel; and it shall come to pass in the last days, saith God, I will pour out of my Spirit upon all flesh: and your sons and your daughters shall prophesy, and your young men shall see visions, and your old men shall dream dreams.
>
> —ACTS 2:16–17

As a part of the church's birthing process two thousand years ago, this outpouring did come. Then the church endured great persecution and extermination until the fourth century when Emperor Constantine made Christianity the church of the state. It was then that the persecution stopped, but the church blended into the ways of the world and Satan. So Martin Luther's reformation provided a bottle to receive the Protestant Reformation's new wine in 1517. And small new wine outpourings splattered here and there until the great Azusa street revivals in 1906 and then again following World War II in the great healing revivals of 1947. And since then, we have seen a proliferation of the Spirit and His gifts, but no one has experienced the earthshaking rumble that first-century church experienced, that is until God pours out His Spirit one final time in this last day before eternity.

THERE'S A WAVE COMING!

I declare to you that there is one last wave of revival that is currently swelling in the realm of the Holy Spirit that will make the Bible's day of Pentecost look like a Sunday school picnic! It is going to break on those who have gathered, as the one hundred twenty in Acts 2 did, to experience its twentieth-century outpouring. But God is not going to have only one hundred twenty this time; He's going to have millions who will participate in this final human drama.

It is going to happen suddenly, just as His outpouring in Acts 2: "And suddenly there came a sound from heaven as of a rushing mighty wind, and it filled all the house where they were sitting" (v. 2).

Suddenly, God is going to spring up churches and rebirth dead churches that have been status quo over the past twenty-five years.

- Suddenly, dysfunctional homes will be put back together.
- Suddenly, miraculous signs will pour out in astounding numbers.
- Suddenly, cripples will walk, the blind will see, and the lost will be found.
- And suddenly, the serving remnant of the church today will awake to a mighty roar of the Spirit that this time will never end.

This coming revival will be a roaring wave of glory that will fill the covenant people of God with miraculous, soulwinning power to harvest the fields of the earth prior to Christ's promised earthly return. It is swelling, and it is coming one day to crash down upon the earth to set the captive free.

HAWAII FIVE-O

The first time I really caught sight of this coming last day's revival coming was when I went on a three-week Asian ministry tour with my pastor, the late Dr. Lester Sumrall. I'll never forget witnessing the dire need and things we saw that I never could have imagined. While in Red China, I had some fun with our tour guide when the subject of food came up using a popular TV commercial line of the time, "Where's the beef?" So one day at one of our stops, our Chinese guide sought to accommodate me, and they served us a plate of gray and white something or other that was rolling around in some rice.

"This is beef?" I asked.

"Yeah, bif! Bif! Dis is bif!" said our guide.

"This is not the kind of bif I'm used to," I said.

So the guide pointed out the window and said "Bif!" again.

I stood up to look where our guide was pointing, and standing outside in a gray rice paddy was some form of pathetic animal that I surmised had to be part of the curse. It had things hanging from its nose, and I could count his ribs. "Bif!" the guide said again, and I dropped the subject.

After three weeks of eating weeds and sticks, we finally arrived in Honolulu, where I made it my mission to find some beef. I set out to find a McDonald's that was located across the street from our hotel. By then I had been with Dr. Sumrall, preaching three times a day, for three weeks, and I wanted to get the taste of weeds and sticks out of my pallet. I wanted some bif! I was in the elevator on my way down to clip through the lobby and across the street to get a hamburger when the elevator door opened, and there stood Dr. Sumrall.

"Turn around, come up stairs, and get dressed; we're going to church!" Dr. Sumrall said. So I turned around, and up we went.

After church Dr. Sumrall told me he would be leaving a day earlier, which meant I would have a day to spend on the island before I left. So the next day I rented a little Suzuki jeep and had my day planned out.

As I was on the beach that day, suddenly I saw the largest waves. These were no ordinary waves, and surfers were braving them. So I said to myself, *I've been to Florida; I can handle these.* I shot out into the water, diving into the waves. But they crashed me to the ocean floor, rolled me over the rocks on the bottom, and buried my face in the sand. When I escaped with my life, I felt as if I had been run through a full Maytag wash cycle. My throat, nose, and ears were gurgling with salt and sand. Water was shooting out of my eyes, and I was bruised and bleeding from crashing against the ocean bottom.

But as I stood on the beach, reeling from the experience, God spoke to me and said this:

"There is a wave coming! A wave of supernatural Holy Ghost power! A wave of unexplainable demonstration of My ability and proof that I am God. There is a demonstration of the Holy Ghost coming! It is coming in a mighty wave, and when it comes, if you are not prepared, it will crush you under its thundering torrents! But if you will get ready, if you will prepare yourself, the wave that will crush others will propel you to the heights and the realms of the demonstration of the glories of My kingdom!"

Then God said, "But you most choose."

I stumbled up to the Suzuki and made a quick dash back to the hotel. That night after I showered, I still had sand in places I didn't know I had. And I was still bleeding, but none of that mattered as I remembered what God had said.

Since that time I've done the best I have been able to do to prepare myself and others for that thundering wave. There is a wave coming that is going to empty hospitals out! There is a wave of glory coming that will anoint ordinary believers with the kind of power that will draw the needy in the world to lay the sick on pallets in their driveways and their front porches in the hopes they will be prayed for when they leave the house for work. I can feel it. I can sense it. That same spirit that raised Jairus's daughter, the widow of Nain's son, Aeneas, and Tabitha will empower the fortified remnant of fathers, mothers, daughters, and sons in these fast-approaching days. It's on the inside of me. And it's in God's Word.

But it's not just me. Revival comes to those eagerly anticipating it. It has been pouring and coming and waving overseas over the past decade. If you don't believe me, just look for the iron curtain and Soviet Communism. When you do, you will find they are gone because of the prayers of the former Soviet bloc church. Also look through the misleading secular press reports at Africa, where revival has been harvesting multiplied thousands over the past twenty years. Look at America. The cloud is the size of a hand, the wind is a breezing rush, but men are taking their places in Christ, and the church is awaking again to our calling in Jesus Christ.

Soon the day will be over when we spurn dependence on the supernatural move of God in our lives. The day is quickly coming to an end when we put on our suits and beautiful dresses to spend an hour and fifteen minutes in church to have our consciences soothed. A dividing line is being drawn as I write today; by the time this is published and in your hands, the divisions will be even more pronounced.

The church of Jesus Christ is coming out of the blur of indistinction caused by our blending with the world. Those of us who are already standing have been labeled the "extreme right" for our moral stands, but our numbers are growing daily. So far our preaching has been for the most part in words of wisdom. But before long, there is going to be a showdown with the demonstration of God's power. God is raising up an army of Elijahs to take on the prophets of Baal, and it won't be the pablum of humanistic doctrine that calls God's fire down from heaven.

The political and religious sides of the fence are shoring up and showing themselves for what they truly are. As the days push on into the darkness to the time of the Antichrist, supernatural power will be the norm. The Antichrist's system and the harlot spoken of in the Book of Revelation won't simply be deceptively spinning the truth to deceive the nations as we now see it. There will be satanic manifestations coming from the Antichrist's camp such as those Moses destroyed when confronting Pharaoh's magicians. Therefore, God will be pouring out His supernatural gifts on His remnant as never seen before.

SLEEPING GIANT

A number of years ago, God's great apostle to the nation of Argentina, Tommy Hicks, saw in a vision this great church awakening as a sleeping giant waking up from a long slumber.

"The greatest gifts that the church of Jesus Christ has ever seen and that have been ever given to the body of Christ do not lie behind us," this rugged apostle said after receiving the three-part vision that changed his life. "They do not lie in the dusty books of past theological rhetoric. They do not lie in the halls of higher education of theology with dust on them two inches deep. Neither do they lie in the Book of Acts. For the church, the greatest giftings, the greatest miracles lie before us. So lift up your eyes and look straight ahead, for the greatest days in the body of Christ lie straight ahead!"[1]

God is drawing from the fringes of His church and from the recesses of the world a people in these last days those who don't care what Dr. So-and-So had to say about the spiritually and politically correct. Their cries will be heard echoing with the shrill cry of John the Baptist preaching, "Repent! For the kingdom of God is nigh! There is no hope in Buddha, Muhammad, New Age, or any other form of godless religion!" Like Jesus, they will be turning over the merchandise tables of the multilevel marketing gurus who have masqueraded as pastors to bring them to their senses.

There are people being called who understand the price and consecration of their salvation as strangers and pilgrims on this earth with heaven on their minds. He is calling a people who, like Abraham, are looking for that city whose architect and builder is God. He is calling a people who, like Caleb, will take Mount Hebron when those surrounding them are cowering in fear. He is calling an army who will be forged in the scorching fires of glory as the spotless bride Paul declares that Jesus will return to wed: "That he might present it to himself a glorious church, not having spot, or wrinkle, or any such thing; but that it should be holy and without blemish" (Eph. 5:27).

NEW WINE OVER TIME

Remember with me now if you could over the past twenty years how we have enjoyed a renaissance of revival in the Word of God. Remember when we began to say, "It is written! No, it is written, devil; you can't take my family. It is written you can't have this preacher. You can't have this revival, Satan, because it is written." And God began to wash us in the water of His Word. Then after He started washing us, He began sending the Holy Ghost to burn the inconsistencies out of us. And He has been doing that, particularly over the past ten years with the iron of pressure, the iron of persecution, to iron our wrinkles out.

Paul said that the Lord will be presented with a church that is without spot or wrinkle. God began to heat up the iron to smooth us out. We went through fallen Christian leaders, and suddenly, to be a Christian was to be connected with scam and shame. But when we came out, we were washed, pressed, and ironed with a new, more balanced view. It stirred up the world, and it stirred up many within our own ranks. Some grew bitter, and some grew better. It all depended upon who chose to climb up on our Father's potter's wheel for counsel and who chose to get caught up in Satan's many accusing siftings.

But now today, a decade later, the remnant of God's host is pressing forward, high over and away from the freeze-dried free coupon giveaway Christianity of the era that promoted selfish lifestyles of ease on the one hand and self-righteous demagoguery on the other. And the Spirit and the bride are saying "Come" to a world that is currently reeling in the vortex of deception and greed. Mammon and lawlessness have taken captive the world of today, and the Spirit is calling a few good women and men to set them free.

I am compelled to share a little more of Tommy Hicks' vision. Joel prophesied men and women would receive such spiritual revelation, and this one given the great Argentine evangelist, who once saw three hundred thousand souls come to the Lord in a single meeting, is a powerful testimony to the end of the age outpouring that's coming our way.

Brother Hicks saw a giant—a picture of the End-Time church. But the giant had been asleep, and his body was covered with debris from head to foot. As Tommy watched it try to arise, thousands of little creatures ran away. When the giant calmed down, the creatures would return. The creatures were demonic strongholds given place through the intermingling sins the church has engaged in through cohabiting with the world. So, this is no time to calm down and chill out, as the world says.

The giant finally found the strength to rise, and it stood up, towering over the clouds. Once standing, the debris was gone. Tommy saw in prophetic type that a cleansing had taken place. A huge remnant had given themselves to Paul's admonition to present their bodies to the Lord as a living sacrifices (Rom. 12:1).

Today, the church is going through the process of being shaped on the Potter's wheel. We are being pressed clean of our wrinkles, and there's much more pressing to do. We are arising from our slumber of selfishness and convenience, and the remnant church is growing slowly, but truly. But it is only happening among those who are refusing to continue blaming the devil or the past for their sin.

This final hour outpouring will come to those who own their sin problem and repent before God, and there is a great move of this currently around our nation.

Sin will surely stop a move of God. It's time to put your foot down, push your plate back, point your finger into the face of the same sin habits for which you have apologized ten thousand times, and say, "In the name of Jesus Christ, I stand in covenant blood, and I refuse from this moment forward to ever allow my mind to even think the thought that would produce the opportunity to commit this sin again!"

There is no place in God's remnant for the "me, my four, and no more" mentality that has us rushing in and out of church as if it were merely another business appointment. There is no place for the "church is so worldly and the world so churchy" social entanglements that have earmarked us in the past.

So, we're going to have to wake up and let the debris fall off. We're going to have to be priests in our homes. We're going to have to be pastors of our jobs. We're going to have to be prophets in our schools. And we're going to have to be evangelists in the streets.

TRUE AMBASSADORS

The remnant are commissioned as ambassadors for Christ to represent Him here on this strange and foreign planet while we await our orders to come home. This is remnant thinking, and the Holy Spirit, who has been in the Father's presence and knows the remedy, will help you do it.

Once the church was cleansed and arose from the filth it slept in, according to Brother Hicks' vision, it experienced a great awakening. Tommy stood amazed as he watched every cloud below the giant's tremendous height become the most glorious shimmering silver he had ever seen. And then the giant began to melt—symbolic of dying to self. It began to sink into the earth as the "look at me" cults of personality began to die.

Finally, Tommy explains, he saw in the Spirit liquid drops of light falling from the sky as rain, until they rose to a flood. Then he saw millions of people arise from the melted form of the giant who began to walk the earth as Christ's miraculous last days harvest church!

Those warming up to the flickering fires of the world's blending will miss this great outpouring. In Tommy's vision, God's church within a church was raising her hands in adoration and praise, and he saw Jesus lay His hands upon her to take His power throughout the earth.

THE WAVE OF THE SPIRIT IS COMING

I can feel the spray of that wave coming now, because I have been preparing. And because I have been preparing, I won't be smashed to the ground by its thundering power. I am going to be part of the remnant, born-again, blood-washed, Holy Ghost filled church against which the gates of our generation shall not prevail.

It's going to take more than padded pews and crystal chandeliers. It's going to take more than a little catechism and prayer. It's going to take an experience in God that the very flames of hell cannot quench! It's going to take everything I've spoken about in this book that enhances your relationship with the Almighty to put you in the kind of relationship where He can bless and fully trust you.

God's potter's wheel is always turning, but only the remnant surrender and report to be formed in His hands. Be forewarned:

Only the remnant are built in battle to endure Satan's siftings and fiery scorchings.

Only God's remnant understand His purpose in their lives and set their mind continually on His things above.

Only the remnant are led by faith to do bold exploits and are trained to recognize Satan's continual, compromising deals (Heb. 5:14).

And only the remnant earnestly seek God's new outpourings of spiritual wine. Their bottles are full of salt and are continually receiving and dispensing the Spirit's blessed flow.

In these quickly waning days approaching the last day before eternity, the Holy Ghost is going to make us a miraculous church. The greatest gifts the church of Jesus Christ has ever seen don't lie behind us in the Book of Acts, or at Azusa Street, or in the healing revivals of the 1940s and 1950s. The greatest days in the body of Christ lie straight ahead! They lie in you!

All God has ever looked for is someone to believe today, someone to believe what they will allow Him to be on any given day. There is no yesterday or tomorrow in the lifestyle of remnant faith. So today is the day of salvation; today is the day of strength.

When Peter bowed to Satan's pressure and warmed himself by the fires of the world's lies and fear, the apostle had no understanding that in just a few short hours he would be talking to the resurrected Christ. Neither did he know that fifty days from then he would be receiving God's miracle power on the day of Pentecost. Satan had convinced the weary apostle that all had been lost and that Jesus was being murdered, never to be seen again.

But Peter had touched, had eaten, and had served with God's living Word. Peter had been instructed of the Lord's resurrection. And when the tempting time arrived, he was sifted, but his heart withstood. He knew the words of Jesus, just as Paul knew God's wisdom, and he was able to consider all things for his sake. So will you, once you enlist in God's End-Time remnant army.

Listen to what the Spirit is saying! The revival we have been hearing about in our bless-me country club sanctuaries is not coming. It is already here. It is growing with God's remnant, and when the time is right, we're going to be drenched.

Today is the day Jesus is looking for you to say *yes* to His calling. Today is the day Jesus wants to empower you to cast out devils, raise the dead, heal the sick, dream His dreams, and see His visions.

Today is the day Jesus is calling you to report to the Potter's wheel, because it is there that He wants to impart His presence to you.

I have tried earnestly to point out the frailties of our human condition as well as the victories God has afforded us over our flesh. As I already stated, I've personally been through times in this calling when the tears streaming down my cheeks were so blinding and my mind was so blocked that I didn't know right from wrong. But I've always been able to pray through to remember the great promises of God's redemption. Like Jeremiah, I've always been able to find my way back the Potter's house, rustle through the messy clay and cuttings that clutter the floor, and climb back up on my Master's wheel to hear His delivering words.

And the work continues. Every time I encounter a new satanic wall, I learn to trust Jesus more than before. I thirst for even newer wine. And that is all God requires of us.

Learn this final lesson from Peter. It is when the resurrected Christ and Pentecost are waiting around life's next corner to bless and empower the Christian that Satan's fires of opposition usually rise to their hottest. This is why people sometimes become the sickest before they're healed and why business looks bleakest the night before the breakthrough. It is within the most perplexing problems and perilous times that the church becomes weak-kneed, often not knowing that in the next days, weeks, or months the greatest blessings we have ever experienced are getting ready to be unleashed. And God is getting ready to unleash!

Satan didn't want Peter to be present with Christ's remnant behind closed doors when Jesus walked through the door of that room (John 20:19–22). And he doesn't want you gathered with God's remnant when God's tidal wave of supernatural power hits or when Jesus comes to rapture us on that final day before eternity. But that is of no consequence to the remnant of God's house. Satan has no power over God's tried and true.

So if you're feeling the heat, just keep cooking. Stay in the kitchen. If you are feeling the pressure, stay on the Potter's wheel. If you are feeling intoxicated, keep drinking of the Spirit. If you are feeling that you've lost control, keep sweetly surrendered to His control.

Continue to stand for righteousness in your home, at your children's school, and in the government of this great land. Because greater is He who is within you than he who is within the world. As you do, God will use you as a precious vessel, sanctified and holy for His own personal use. Jesus will confirm your ministry with signs following. And one day soon, Jesus will welcome you home into everlasting habitations with the coveted affirmation, "Well done, good and faithful servant; you have been faithful over a few things, I will make you ruler over many things. Enter into the joy of your Lord."

> Not by might, nor by power, but by my spirit, saith the LORD of hosts.
>
> —ZECHARIAH 4:6

THIRTEEN

THE PARTY OF
THE AGES

*And Jesus returned in the power of the Spirit into Galilee: and
there went out a fame of him through all the region round about.
And he taught in their synagogues, being glorified of all. And he
came to Nazareth, where he had been brought up: and, as his
custom was, he went into the synagogue on the sabbath day, and
stood up for to read. And there was delivered unto him the book
of the prophet Esaias. And when he had opened the book, he
found the place where it was written, The Spirit of the Lord is
upon me, because he hath anointed me to preach the gospel to the
poor; he hath sent me to heal the brokenhearted, to preach deliverance to the captives, and recovering of sight to the blind, to set
at liberty them that are bruised, to preach the acceptable year of
the Lord.*

—LUKE 4:14–19

The day before eternity is a jubilee day. It's that final party where
every debt is paid and the spirit of heaviness is exchanged for the
garment of joy. The last day before eternity is party time. Jesus
announced the coming party when He read Isaiah 61 in the
Nazareth synagogue in the hearing of all the religious people of the
region.

Jesus returned in the power of the Spirit into Galilee, and there went out a fame of him throughout the region. He taught in their synagogue, being glorified of all, and came to Nazareth, where he had grown up as a child. He went to the synagogue on the Sabbath, and He was given the book of the prophet Isaiah. Reading from Isaiah 61, Jesus proclaimed the *acceptable year of the Lord.* What is that year? It's Jubilee; it's party time; it's now!

Centuries before, Isaiah by the Spirit of God knew the psyche of Jesus through the prophetic gift. You understand that it was David who was able prophetically to see as a seer the psyche of the Son of God as He hung between heaven and earth, suspended between two worlds. David through the Spirit understood His psyche and began to declare the mind of Christ on the cross.

Isaiah now ascends into the prophetic realm and begins to have revealed unto him more than Jesus just articulated with speech in Luke 4. If you want to get the entire message, read Isaiah 61. Jesus used Isaiah 61 to frame His ministry and to proclaim prophetically the day before eternity.

What happens during the acceptable year of the Lord?

- Good news comes to the meek.
- Healing mends broken hearts.
- Captives are set free.
- Bondages are broken.
- Mourners are comforted.
- Beauty replaces ashes.
- Those wearing the spirit of heaviness are clothed with the garment of praise.

I asked God the meaning of "beauty for ashes." God revealed that the ashes represent those things in life that are perishable and that seem worthless to us. Those things that once burned brightly in the fiery, passionate love for Christ are now only ashes.

I see in this the institutional church, the cult of religious Christianity in the ashes. In this final day the cult will die and God will resurrect the *ecclesia.*

Those in the institutional, cultic church have been yoked by cultural influences, but the yoke will be destroyed by the anointing of the Lord that Jesus proclaimed through Isaiah 61.

There is a party happening in Christ's church. Are you a part of it? Some in today's religious church have become comfortable with poverty, being brokenhearted, and remaining bound by religion. But in this glorious army marching into eternity's dawn, we are living in Jubilee. Jesus is throwing a party for us. The blind see, and the lame dance. Are you partying? It's the acceptable year of the Lord.

When Jesus declared that Isaiah's prophecy had been fulfilled in their midst, the religious folks led Him to the brow of the hill where the city was built so that they might cast Him down headlong. But He passed through the midst of them and went His way.

Religious people hate parties. They love keeping people bound in religious legalism. They want people poor, brokenhearted, and overshadowed with the spirit of heaviness. But Jesus was announcing a party, and they wanted nothing to do with Him or His celebration. The religious keep everyone in debt, but Jubilee sets the debtors free. It's the last day before eternity. The acceptable year of the Lord, Jubilee, is here! Let's party!

From the dawn of creation, every country, culture, and creed has found cause for celebration. From Independence Day to Christmas Day, we prepare for the pomp and the circumstance of the occasion. Though parties have punctuated our heritage, they've also become an exclamation point to a loose-living, sin-infected society. Take, for example, a young Nazarite by the name of Samson.

Seduced by sin, Samson laid his head in the lap of Delilah. He told her the secret of his power, and the end result was a party thrown by the enemy Philistines.

Belshazzar, king of Babylon, decided to throw a party. Intoxicated upon his own persona and glory, he drank from the sanctified golden goblets of God in defiance of Jehovah. He was weighed in the balance and found wanting. His party came to an abrupt end when his enemies destroyed his kingdom.

Herod decided to throw a party in honor of his adulteress wife. Drunken and yielding to the seductions of her teenage, virgin daughter who danced before him, Herod cried out, "Anything you want is yours, up to the half of my kingdom." Her request was the head of John the Baptist on a silver platter.

The parties of this world also end in disaster. But Jesus invites us to a party that will last for eternity.

The world loves a party, but it cannot find any celebration that will turn ashes into beauty and replace the spirit of heaviness with a garment of praise. Even Pentecostals and Charismatics have tried to throw bogus parties with their shouting, dancing, and rituals of praise. But there's one party that's worth going to, and it lasts through the night and into the dawn of eternity. The King of glory is throwing this party for the bride and the Bridegroom. Are you coming to the party?

Jesus is the life of this party. The curtain is rising on the last act of human drama. The proclamations have been published. The invitations have all been sent out, and they read, "Let all who will come." The stage is set. The participants are all in place. The time is now, and the place is here. Jehovah God tonight stands guard over our celebration. It's party time, and the drink of the party is new wine.

You may be yoked in bondage and feel that you cannot attend the party. What yokes you . . . what keeps you from the party? The yoke is not addiction. The yoke is not perversion. The yoke is not sexual immorality.

Have you noticed that those in the world's parties appear happier and more prosperous than those professing to know Jesus? Why is that? They still cower and stumble under the heaviest yoke of all: *the spirit of heaviness.* This yoke denies the promise of the One who throws the party:

> And ye now therefore have sorrow: but I will see you again, and your heart shall rejoice, and your joy no man taketh from you. And in that day ye shall ask me nothing. Verily, verily, I say unto you, Whatsoever ye shall ask the Father in my name, he will give it you. Hitherto have ye asked nothing in my name: ask, and ye shall receive, that your joy may be full.
>
> —JOHN 16:22–24

In the *ecclesia* a paradigm shift, a strategic inflection point as one Intel Corporation executive calls it, has occurred. In religion, everyone is bound, poor, and sad. In the true church of Jesus Christ, a real party is happening; the religious folks cannot stand it. Every fresh new golden era of human history has always been directly preceded by the devotion and righteous passion of one or more individuals who knew their God and knew where they were going. I did not say they knew *about Him.* I said they knew *Him.* In the *ecclesia,* the saints know the King. So what's needed for us to participate in His party? What are the ingredients that make for a party in this day before eternity?

SOMEONE MUST DECLARE, "IT'S PARTY TIME!"

The key ingredient that turns the key in the lock to open up the blessing of Jubilee is a priest who declares the Year of Jubilee. In Leviticus 25 the high priest took the shofar and sounded the decree that Jubilee had begun, the fiftieth year had arrived, and all bondages were broken and debts forgiven. Jubilee is the acceptable year of the Lord. The captives are set free.

Now is the acceptable year of the Lord. It's time that every prisoner went free. It's the time when God chooses to be God all by Himself. It is the year when joy overtakes your burden. It is the year when every yoke is destroyed. It is the year when your family is getting put back together. It is the year when your debt is being canceled. Jesus has declared your Jubilee. It's time to party. So what's the next ingredient to having a party?

IT MUST BE TIME FOR A PARTY

You can't throw a party unless people know the time. Whoever announces a party must also proclaim the time and place of the party. "This is the acceptable year of the Lord." Now is the time for the party, and this—the *ecclesia* of Christ—is the place!

In 1948 the Cleveland Indians won the World Series. But something more important happened in 1948. A nation was born in Palestine, the nation of Israel. At that moment the clock started ticking. God's countdown to Jubilee began. Seven times seven years, forty-nine years, and on the fiftieth year you shall proclaim Jubilee. Now we are in a natural Jubilee for Israel. But I have better news for you than that. We are in a spiritual Jubilee in Christ.

After Jesus proclaimed the acceptable year of the Lord, He then "closed the book." Jesus then announced, "This day is this scripture fulfilled in your ears" (Luke 4:21). Some received what He said and entered into it, but others rejected His proclamation and did not receive God's garment of praise.

It's Jubilee when you receive a revelation of who Jesus is for yourself. God spoke to me. He took me back to when Dr. Sumrall had handed out little scribbled pieces of paper. God had met with him at midnight and spoken to him until five in the morning. He handed me those papers and began to weep. He said, "You read them; I can't read them."

The first line of that revelation read, "It's almost midnight." We are in the final hour before midnight. It was midnight when Samson lifted the gates of the city. It was midnight in the jail cell as Paul and Silas sang, and heaven couldn't help but hear their call. It was midnight when Boaz was revealed to Ruth, her kinsman redeemer. It's midnight. I have a revelation for you from the King: Midnight approaches . . . are you ready?

It's midnight in North Korea. Eighty-two percent of the children in North Korea tonight are malnourished; over 50 percent are not expected to live through the next twelve months. One-third of the population, if something doesn't happen, will starve to death in the next nine months. A hungry belly knows no politics.

It's time for a party. They're shredding tree bark in North Korea and selling it in the marketplace for food. We spent more last year on Diet Coke than some Third World countries will spend on their entire economy. Don't you understand? This is the time and place to declare Jubilee. The church of Jesus Christ is marching through this day, setting captives free and starting a party that will last for eternity. Are you coming to the party?

GET DRESSED FOR THE PARTY!

In this acceptable year of the Lord, this time of Jubilee, we need to put on the right attire for the party. What is it? *The garment of praise.*

The literal translation of Isaiah 61:3 is "I will cover you with celebration for the spirit of hopelessness." God has declared that He will set ambushes for our enemies (2 Chron. 20). What are we to do at the party? "Then they returned, every man of Judah and Jerusalem, and Jehoshaphat in the forefront of them, to go again to Jerusalem with joy; for the LORD had made them to rejoice over their enemies. And they came to Jerusalem with psalteries and harps and trumpets unto the house of the LORD" (2 Chron. 20:27–28).

The battle belongs to the Lord. Put on the garment of praise and begin to thank God for the victory.

EVERY PARTY HAS REFRESHMENTS

You can't put new wine in old skins. You cannot let the past dictate your future. You can't pray as you've been praying. You can't shout as you've been shouting. You can't praise as you've been praising. You can't sing as you've been singing. You can't preach as you've been preaching. It's a new day for a new people to shout a new shout of victory and destroy the gates of hell! Are you thirsty for some new wine?

What will we eat at the party? Are you hungry, really hungry for God? Are you hungering and thirsting after righteousness? What are you feeding your spirit in this last day before eternity?

One of the first things my dear friend Kenneth Copeland ever taught me was that if I was going to feed my natural body natural food, I also needed to feed my spirit man spiritual food. Copeland confided, "I was in a great crusade, and I looked out over the congregation, and God opened my eyes. I saw emaciated bodies. I saw eyes sunk back in heads. I saw the wave of God come, and those bodies try to lift their hands, but they couldn't—they were too weak. I said, 'God, what's going on?' He said that it was the condition of their spirits, for they were spending no time feeding on spirit food."

What are you going to eat at this party? The Lamb of God will feed you. "For the Lamb which is in the midst of the throne shall feed them, and shall lead them unto living fountains of waters: and God shall wipe away all tears from their eyes" (Rev. 7:17). We eat of His flesh and drink His blood. John 6:54–57 declares:

> Whoso eateth my flesh, and drinketh my blood, hath eternal life; and I will raise him up at the last day. For my flesh is meat indeed, and my blood is drink indeed. He that eateth my flesh, and drinketh my blood, dwelleth in me, and I in him. As the living Father hath sent me, and I live by the Father: so he that eateth me, even he shall live by me.

On the last day, we will feast on the Word of God.

PARTY TIME IS HOUSECLEANING TIME!

Turn off television. Stop playing video games. Put away your recreational or sporting toys. It's time to clean house. A Jewish father during Passover was commanded to take a branch of hyssop and sweep the house. What was he sweeping out? Before we can party, we must clean house. It's time to get rid of the leaven of the Pharisees with their external religious show (Matt. 16:6). Professional church people must change or leave.

David prayed, "Purge me with hyssop, and I shall be clean: wash me, and I shall be whiter than snow" (Ps. 51:7). Jesus is returning for a pure and spotless bride. His *ecclesia* must be swept clean of the leaven of legalism, religion, and tradition.

It's time to clean the house for His party. Away with legalism, manipulation, control, intimidation, and religious self-righteousness. Nothing will make His body clean but His blood. The anointing prepares the house for the party. It's the anointing of His blood. Paint it on the doorposts of the church. Rub it into the hearts of every believer. Cover the whole body with the blood of Jesus, cleansing away all leaven. It's party time, so get your house in order.

HAVING A PARTY? WHO'S PAYING THE TAB?

We have every reason to party. The tab, the bill, has been paid. God's justice had demanded that the price must be paid. Blood must be shed sufficient enough to heal the wounds and forgive the transgressions of all humanity. Jesus paid the price.

The ringing of the hammer was heard on Calvary some two thousand years ago, and nails parted sinew and flesh. Jesus' muscles jerked and quaked, nerves quivered and shook. His tongue, swollen out of His mouth, spoke forgiveness from a cross. His side made a perfect target for a Roman centurion's sword. Water and blood gushed forth when the soldier pierced Jesus' side. We were washed in His blood and cleansed from every sin.

Jesus paid the price with His blood on the cross for your party and mine. What a reason to shout! What a reason to celebrate with joy! Forgiven, cleansed by the blood of Jesus. Of course, we must party, and party we will—for eternity!

When the Roman legions would conquer a nation, their conqueror would ride on a chariot, dragging behind him the conquered slaves with chains and ropes through the streets of Rome. All the citizens rejoiced and partied; they wildly applauded their conquering king. Why do you remain seated in your church pew? What keeps you anchored to your couch? How can you just sit around when the clock is ticking, the final day is winding down, and the King is marching through the streets in victory?

Coming over the horizon of this last day rides our King on a white horse. He has won the victory. Stay mired in the mud of your own battles if you must, but I'm going to a party, and you're invited. Get out of the miry clay and set your feet upon the rock of Jesus. Praise Him, the marching King who has conquered death and the grave. "O death, where is thy sting? O grave, where is thy victory? The sting of death is sin; and the strength of sin is the law. But thanks be to God, which giveth us the victory through our Lord Jesus Christ" (1 Cor. 15:55–57).

STRIKE UP THE BAND . . .
TURN UP THE MUSIC . . . IT'S PARTY TIME!

At Jesus' party, joyful music will shatter the eardrums of the religious deaf and will loose the tongues of spiritual mutes. Stop playing funeral music! Burn the woolen, winter garments of heaviness. Put on the garments of praise. Set your feet to dancing and your hands to clapping. Shout! The King of glory is throwing the greatest party that eternity will ever witness.

> Praise ye the LORD. Sing unto the LORD a new song, and his praise in the congregation of saints. Let Israel rejoice in him that made him: let the children of Zion be joyful in their King. Let them praise his name in the dance: let them sing praises unto him with the timbrel and harp. For the LORD taketh pleasure in his people: he will beautify the meek with salvation. Let the saints be joyful in glory: let them sing aloud upon their beds. Let the high praises of God be in their mouth, and a two-edged sword in their hand; to execute vengeance upon the heathen, and punishments upon the people; to bind their kings with chains, and their nobles with fetters of iron; to execute upon them the judgment written: this honour have all his saints. Praise ye the LORD.
>
> —PSALM 149:1–9

Our conquering King has taken back for you everything the adversary has stolen out of your life—your dreams, hopes, future, and your family. His blood has purchased your salvation and your healing—by His stripes you are healed. The captives have been set free from generational curses. He was bruised for your iniquity. You are delivered from sin and death. So put on the garment of praise.

YOU ARE CORDIALLY INVITED TO HIS PARTY

You're cordially invited to the party of the ages. Don't miss the procession partying in the streets and following the conquering King. The terrible army of God, marching under the banner of Christ, thunders toward the midnight of time. Soon, eternity will dawn. Will you be weeping as an observer or partying as a participant?

God's clock is ticking. Time is expiring. Will you be prepared for eternity's party with the Bridegroom?

THE DAY BEFORE
ETERNITY

The lazy ignore it.
The wicked dread it.
The foolish deny it.
The reprobates teach against it.
The intellectual liberals rationalize it.
The ungodly want to delay it.
The mockers laugh at it.
And the religious hope against hope that they don't miss it.

"Watch therefore; for ye know not what hour your Lord doth come" (Matt. 24:42).

How are you sleeping at night?

Do you rest well, knowing that your day was filled with the Lord, or does a restlessness pervade your nights, causing you to wake up in cold sweats gripped by the icy tentacles of fear?

Like it or not, history avalanches around you toward the precipice of eternity. As quickly as a blink, the end could overtake you. Are you ready?

At this very moment, the final day of history unfolds around us. Prophetic imagery framed history within the six days that God created the universe. For six days God created, then He rested. For six days history would unwind, and on the seventh day, human beings would enter either into God's eternal rest or hell's unending torture.

We live in the final hours of *the day before eternity!* The day before the end!

For each of us, life is but a day passing quickly in the sands of time. The ancient Hebrews reckoned time each day by twelve hours. Jesus affirmed, "Are there not twelve hours in the day? If any man walk in the day, he stumbleth not, because he seeth the light of this world. But if a man walk in the night, he stumbleth, because there is no light in him" (John 11:9–10).

The division of the day into twelve-hour periods came from the era of the Babylonian captivity. So the sixth hour was noon, and the twelfth hour was midnight. History plummets madly into midnight unaware that the Judge is coming, bringing in His hands the scales of eternal judgment.

The Lord is coming again . . . soon! Jesus warned us to gird our loins, keep our lights burning, be ready, and watch for the Bridegroom. As His bride, we must be alert and prepared (Luke 12:35–36). "Remember therefore how thou has received and heard, and hold fast, and repent. If therefore thou shalt not watch, I will come on thee as a thief, and thou shalt not know what hour I will come upon thee" (Rev. 3:3).

It's approaching midnight. Are you prepared to receive your Bridegroom and His blessing? Or will you be caught sleeping and lacking? For the ancient Hebrews, the night was divided into four watches. The final watch approaches. Are you prepared and ready?

Jesus said, "Blessed are those servants, whom the lord when he cometh shall find watching: verily I say unto you, that he shall gird himself, and make them to sit down to meat, and will come forth and serve them. And if he shall come in the second watch, or come in the third watch, and find them so, blessed are those servants. . . . Be ye therefore ready also: for the Son of man cometh at an hour when ye think not" (Luke 12:37–38, 40).

A greeter stands shaking hands at the church door, and an usher sees people to their seats. One is ready, and one is not.

A preacher pours with sweat proclaiming the kingdom of God

while a teacher guides students through the letters of Paul. One's ready, and one's not.

A Promise Keeper shouts cheers in a stadium while a housekeeper hums along with the praise songs playing on her CD player. One may be ready, and one may not.

One works in the field alongside another. One is ready, and one is not. Which one are you? Ready or not?

A husband reads his devotional while a wife watches her favorite Christian program. One may be ready, and one may not.

One church languishes through its style and tradition while the church, the *ecclesia,* marches through the final day before eternity ushering into history the revolution of God's glory, river, fire, and presence.

This book is both a warning and a preparation. In the final hours of this day before time finally ceases, you must get ready, stay prepared, and be doing the work of the Lord.

This book is a wake-up call to the church. No longer is the church an institution, for she has been called out (*ecclesia*) of this world and into the kingdom of light.

This book is also a life manual, your guide for End-Time living. In the pages that you have just read, you have seen:

- How to repent and surrender totally to Jesus.
- How the Lord will shape you on the Potter's wheel.
- How to be equipped for the spiritual battles you face.
- How Satan will attack you and how your faith will be refined by fire.
- How to pray through every trial and tribulation in life.
- How you will be led by the Spirit through trust and faith.
- How to overcome the temptation to make a deal with the enemy.
- How to arrive in heaven while forsaking hell.
- How to live victoriously in the End Times and how to drink new wine.
- How to prepare for the final awakening of the church.
- How to fight in God's army that revolutionarily dismantles the religious systems of this world.

- How to make changes in your life that will count for eternity.

Gazing through the portals of heaven, you will see the Bridegroom dressing as He dances with joy, anticipating His wedding with the bride. A marriage feast is being prepared, and the garlands of everlasting flowers grace the river of life flowing from His throne. All the wedding preparations are entering the final day.

The hours tumble toward the twelfth and final hour of midnight and toward eternal life beyond this world. A rapture and resurrection are coming. As a thief in the night, the Groom will return to some waiting and ready, while others sleep.

This book sounds the clarion blasts of warning. Are you awake, ready, and waiting? Or are you asleep? Be forewarned, you are living in . . .

The day before eternity.

How will you respond to the warning of this prophet?

Like a voice crying in the wilderness, the solitary prophet cries out . . . It's the last day, the final hour before eternity.
A remnant, revolutionary church stirs.
A slumbering giant stirs to drink once more from the cup of new wine.
A fresh wind is blowing.
Lost, thirsty, and hungry millions lift their heads, hoping to hear a final word of grace before the gates of hell close behind them, imprisoning their souls forever.
Is anyone listening?

Are you listening?

God calls His End-Time army to suit up with His armor and stand firm against the most ferocious attacks in history from the enemy.

Some will opt to stay in the camp, warming themselves by a fire and claiming they do not know the Commander in Chief.

But others will heed the call and discover eternity's greatest reward—the saving of millions of souls.

Indeed, it is the final day and the last hour.

What you do will not only determine how you will spend eternity, but also how your family, your friends, your town, and even your enemies will spend eternity.

Before you go through eternity's turnstile, will you radically surrender to Christ?

Before stepping onto eternity's escalator, will you stay on the Potter's wheel until He finishes shaping you?

Before walking into the refreshing eternal presence of Christ, will you first go through the Refiner's fire?

Before receiving your eternal gift, will you first use the gifts you have been given to build the kingdom of God in this final hour?

Before hearing "well done, good and faithful servant," will you become a servant—body, mind, and soul conformed to the image of Jesus?

Before yielding to the temptation to retreat, will you revolt against all that this world represents and march with the King of glory into the eternal dawn of His kingdom?

Eternity beckons, but the night still lingers for a final moment. Redeem the time while time still exists. Make every second count for eternity.

It's the last day...the final hour...and the waning minutes before the dawn of a new day and the end of this age!

Now is your day before eternity.

▓ Notes

Two
Shaped on the Potter's Wheel

1. *Spurgeon at His Best,* compiled by Tom Carter (Grand Rapids, MI: Baker Book House, 1990), p. 102.
2. "Have Thine Own Way, Lord," words by Adelaide A. Pollard, music by George C. Stebbins. Public domain.

Three
Crossing the Victor's Line

1. Martin Luther King, Jr., *The Strength to Love* (New York: Harper & Row, 1963), p. 20.
2. The examples given are from the book *Pursuit of Excellence* by Ted Engstrom (Grand Rapids, MI: Zondervan Publishing House, 1982).
3. *That Incredible Christian Essay: The Christian Life Is Not Easy,* compiled by Anita M. Bailey (Camp Hill, PA: Christian Publishing, n.d.), pp. 72–73. The actual quote reads: "The average Christian these days is a harmless enough thing. . . . He is a child wearing with considerable self-consciousness the harness of the warrior; he is a sick eaglet that can never mount up with wings; he is a spent pilgrim who has given up the journey and sits with a waxy smile trying to get what pleasure he can from sniffing the wilted flowers he has plucked by the way. . . . He [Satan] has succeeded in weakening their resolution, neutralizing their convictions, and taming their original urge to do exploits; now they are little more than statistics that contribute financially to the upkeep of the religious institution. . . . My point here is that if we want to escape the struggle we have but to draw back and accept the currently accepted low-keyed Christian life as the normal one. That is all Satan wants. That will ground our power,

stunt our growth, and render us harmless to the kingdom of darkness. Compromise will take the pressure off. Satan will not bother a man who has quit fighting. But the cost of quitting will be a life of peaceful stagnation."

EIGHT
DON'T DEAL WITH THE DEVIL

1. "A Mighty Fortress Is Our God," words and music by Martin Luther. Public domain.

NINE
HEAVENLY CITIZENSHIP

1. D. L. Moody, *Heaven* (New York: Revell, 1980), p. 18.

TWELVE
THE FINAL AWAKENING

1. This three-part vision by Tommy Hicks occurred on July 25, 1961. It is related on pages 48–53 in *Dreams and Visions of History and Prophecy,* revised and enlarged by Dr. Lester Sumrall (South Bend, IN: LeSea Publishing Company, 1990).

For more information about *Breakthrough,* World Harvest church, or to receive a product list of the many books and audio and video tapes by Rod Parsley, write or call:

BREAKTHROUGH
P. O. Box 32932
Columbus, OH 43232-0932
614-837-4088

For information about World Harvest Bible College, write or call:

WORLD HARVEST BIBLE COLLEGE
P. O. Box 32901
Columbus, OH 43232-0901
614-837-4088

If you need prayer, the *Breakthrough*
prayer line is open 24 hours a day, 7 days a week.

614-837-3232

Visit Rod Parsley at his web site address:
www.breakthrough.net